CW00494489

# The Schoolmaster

A commentary upon the aims and methods
of an assistant-master in a public school.

## Arthur Christopher Benson

*'Le travail, il n'y a que ça!'*

Published by
Peridot Press
2011

**This edition published 2011**

by Peridot Press,
12 Deben Mill Business Centre, Old Maltings Approach,
Melton, Woodbridge, Suffolk IP12 1BL
Tel: 01394 389850 Fax: 01394 386893
Email: enquiries@johncatt.com
Website: www.johncatt.com

**ISBN: 978 1 908095 30 5**
**eISBN: 978 1 908095 32 9**

Set and designed by Peridot Press

Printed by Dolman Scott
www.dolmanscott.co.uk

From Wellington to Orwell, Shelley to Cameron the names of distinguished Old Etonians form a rich roll call of British national life. Yet only one man has his name recorded on a commemorative blue plaque on a school building. That man is A C Benson.

The plaque, erected by the Windsor and Eton Society on Godolphin House, marks Benson as the House Master of that place, but with a greater flourish cites him as the author of *Land of Hope and Glory*. Such a celebration captures a headline but reveals so little of the man. How, then, shall I extol him? Benson was a man of many parts, but above all he was a consummate schoolmaster, dedicated, stimulating, idealistic yet wise to the ways of the world, and more particularly to the wiles and needs of teenage schoolboys. His book *The Schoolmaster* is personal and idiosyncratic and remains one of the best accounts of schoolmastering that has been written. I am delighted to see this work back in print, which for A C Benson is the most fitting memorial.

*Tony Little*
*Head Master, Eton College*

# INTRODUCTION

BY JONATHAN SMITH

In 1997, browsing in a second hand bookshop in Brecon, I reached up to a high shelf and pulled down a small fading brown volume. Not that the title in itself, *The Schoolmaster*, was all that promising. I was on holiday and only too glad to be away for a while from my classroom and, in the way one is, glad also to have a break from some of my rather too schoolmasterly colleagues. Nor, I admit to my shame, had I heard of the author, A C Benson.

I opened the front cover and looked at the publication date: 1902. The pencilled price (£2 ) was, however, bang in the middle of my range, so to catch more light I took the book to the shop window and read for a bit to see if I was prepared to buy it. Within seconds I was smiling at the first sentence:

> I think it must be conceded at the outset that there clings about the profession of schoolmastering a certain slight social disability.

Nice, ouch, nicely put. A few pages further in and I was nodding as I got to this:

> A brisk, idle man with a knack of exposition and the art of clear statement can be a scandalously effective teacher.

True, too true, and lovely use of the word 'scandalously'. When the writer moved on to the importance of discipline I was not sure if I was smiling or wincing:

> The power of maintaining discipline is the *unum necessarium* for a teacher… It insults the soul, it is destructive of all self-respect and dignity to be incessantly at the mercy of boys.

They are merciless, and the pathos of the situation never touches them at all.

And by the time my eye landed on this passage 'on work' and drudgery I was thinking, please, can we have this man as the Minister for Education, and can we have him *now*:

> The conclusion is that it is not a self-indulgence, but a plain duty, for masters to keep themselves fresh and active-minded; and the spirit in which a man allows himself to be carried helplessly down in a stream of mechanical duties is not only not praiseworthy, but highly reprehensible.

What exactly had captured me? It was, I think, three things. The dry, if not sly, humour; the delightfully fluent style in which he made telling observations in the lightest of ways; but above all the sense that here was an experienced and perceptive man who knew his profession inside out, an observant man who understood the human pressures and subtle complexities of the school world in which he lived, and a world in which I hoped (but doubted) that one hundred years later I still did.

*** 

Arthur Benson (1862-1925) spent his life at the heart of three influential and interconnecting circles: the church, the academic world and the literary scene. He lived, that is, amongst the great and the good of late Victorian and Edwardian England. Though it is not a word he would have used, he was an Establishment figure. As for the Bensons themselves, they were a multi-talented, distinguished and creative family; they were also a deeply troubled, manic-depressive and dysfunctional family. There were six children, two of whom died young, and the four who survived were 'all awfully clever' and 'unpermissibly gifted' though not, in another phrase of the time, the marrying kind.

Their mother, Mary, 'and the greatest blessing' of Arthur's life, fell passionately in love with a number of women in the course of her marriage, and in her widowhood enjoyed the life she preferred with her own sex. In 1862 Mary gave birth to her second son, Arthur, in Wellington College where her dominating husband Edward Benson (later to be the Bishop of Truro and then the Archbishop of Canterbury) had been appointed the first Master. Arthur's first breath, then, was taken in a school which was to be his home for eleven years, and he was to breathe the air of schools and colleges for the rest of his life. Teaching was in his blood.

If we reduce A C Benson's CV to a few bare facts this is what we find: a boy at Eton, on to read classics at King's College, Cambridge, back to Eton to teach classics for 20 years (13 of them as a housemaster), then 20 years back at Cambridge as an unpaid don, this time at Magdalene College, in which his last ten were spent as Master of the college to which he proved a great benefactor.

Unusual for a schoolmaster and a don, Arthur Benson had an important and successful life beyond the school walls and the college windows. He was a compulsive and prolific writer, so much so that he was sometimes accused of being fatally fluent: there was a Punch cartoon in 1906, which ran: 'Self-denial week: Mr. A.C.Benson refrains from publishing a book.' He brought out well over 50 in all, many of them big sellers if unworthy of his gifts; increasingly at home in grand social circles, he edited Queen Victoria's letters; he filled 180 volumes of a very private diary, and he wrote the words of *Land of Hope and Glory*.

Yet his life, outwardly approved or not, was far from easy. He suffered from severe depressions and, while teaching at Eton, he had a major breakdown. He had never let himself go – and then he cracked. While it may be scant comfort to those who suffer in this way, it is true that great work often comes out of unresolved personalities, and all too often being well adjusted has little to do with creativity. Immensely hard-working and hypersensitive to any criticism, Arthur could be very sharp about others as well as being devastatingly waspish in his diaries, though to be fair he was also unsparing in his analysis of himself.

With his tightly controlled emotions, he was the sort of teacher who, I suspect, would feel threatened by the appearance of another adult in his classroom, the kind of teacher who is biased in favour of his own pupils, and the kind of housemaster who resented any adverse comments on anyone in his house. Some who are reading that description may well be nodding in recognition of this Common Room type. Yet he was a man of many qualities and many virtues and deeply loved by the boys in Benson's. 'There is not a boy in the house,' one said later, 'who would not rather be punished by any other master than be spoken to by you.' They were all proud to be in his care, he understood them in an uncanny way, and he followed their later lives with pride.

His romantic sensitivity to his pupils would no doubt today be seen as a sign of repressed homosexuality. I do not know the nature of Arthur Benson's homosexuality, nor the line that he trod. What matters to me is the wisdom he has to pass on to us now, some of which you will find in these pages. As his superb biographer David Newsome – himself to become Master of Wellington College in 1980 – wrote, 'Arthur Benson was a romantic; he was also a realist: a good combination, I would say, for a successful housemaster.'

A good combination, I would argue, for all who would wish to be successful teachers in any school at any time.

\*\*\*

Picking Benson's *The Schoolmaster* off that shelf in 1997, and reading his words on how we might best go about our jobs, could not have come at a more timely moment for me. For 20 years or more our profession had been turned upside down by a misguided mindset based on an accountability framework and fuelled by an inappropriately industrial way of looking at teaching. For all those years, with many of them as a head of department, I had been required to read piles of dreadful pamphlets and target driven documents (comically called 'educational literature') and then been urged to 'cascade' these 'model' views of 'best practice' over all those in my department.

Quite often, quite simply, and quite seriously, I did even not understand what these people were writing about. What did these words *mean*? And what was I to do? I could barely cut a path to the novels and plays and poems on my shelves because the floor of my office was covered with piles of assessment data or badly expressed statements of the obvious. There was a near fatal mismatch developing between what we were being told to do and what the best teachers were doing and had always done. Like many in classrooms up and down the country I was struggling to hold on to what I believed were lasting truths, and, even worse, I was on the edge of a disillusionment that I feared would badly affect the way I taught, if not end my career.

During those years my daughter – after hearing one of my evening rants or seeing me head in hands mumbling dangerously – would often suggest that I stopped complaining and started to write down what I felt mattered in teaching, that in effect I started to fight back, that I did a bit of counter-punching from the chalk face, but I always replied that no one would be interested and least of all any publisher.

After reading Benson's *The Schoolmaster*, though, I began to feel some strength returning, and then my resolve hardening.

What was wrong with writing about our profession in simple English? That's what Benson did. That's what we should all do. Indeed, what was better than trying to write about a difficult thing like teaching in simple English? If Benson, in his study in 1902, could make me enjoy reading about and thinking about our job perhaps I could, a century later, make some of my generation feel the same. Perhaps I could write about a schoolteacher's life in the way that rang bells and put a spring in the step? Perhaps I could even make the readers smile, nod, wince, laugh and feel a little bit better about themselves. Best of all, perhaps I could make some want to join our profession.

So, I would never have written *The Learning Game*, nor, come to that, *The Following Game*, without the inspiring example of A C Benson. It would be melodramatic to say that coming across this book saved me, but it certainly cheered me up and helped me to turn a corner. Some might well call *The Schoolmaster* old-fashioned but I don't mind that. A lot of things called old-fashioned are in effect simply out of fashion.

Not that I agree with every word Benson writes or share all his views. Of course I don't. No two teachers ever agree about how their job is best done, and besides there are so many ways of being good at it. Some bits of Benson make me feel uncomfortable. For example I do not like his use of the word 'evil'. There are also a few paragraphs I would like to cut. Yes, that would make a short book even shorter, but then I am beginning to find that I agree with Chekhov when he said: 'Everything I read now seems not short enough.'

I am delighted that Peridot Press are reprinting this brief, wise, amusing, clear, sensitive and subtle classic.

# PREFACE

The following pages do not profess to be a scientific educational treatise; they merely aim at considering the life of the schoolmaster from within. It seems a pity that one who has exercised the profession of a schoolmaster for a good many years should make no attempt to gather up and record experience; it is useful simply to compare impressions; and though the following is merely a personal view, and lays claim to no sort of scientific or philosophical treatment, yet it may be of interest to other teachers, and may even be of use to those who have not yet begun their professional life, but are looking forward to joining the ranks of the profession.

The schoolmaster is perhaps not so much criticised at present as he ought to be; or such criticism is of a secret character. The public schools of England just now enjoy a considerable popularity, rightly or wrongly, in the country; but what is still needed is that schoolmasters should have a more definite aim, a theory of their art, and it seems a pity that so many of us schoolmasters do our work in so fortuitous a way. I therefore venture to gather up the fruits of my experience, and to try to uphold, not boldly but sedately, the dignity of the profession to which I have given my best years.

*Omnibus Adiutoribus*

# Contents

# I

# INTRODUCTORY

I think it must be conceded at the outset that there clings about the profession of schoolmastering a certain slight social disability; it is regarded as one of the less liberal of the liberal professions:* it is not a profession which, to use a vile phrase, 'leads to' anything in particular; that is to say, it is not held to be a profession for a very capable or ambitious man. This is not necessarily a low point of view. Ambition is a fine quality, and a man who is conscious of ability and power, who holds energetic views, who has decided proclivities, who becomes aware that his own views influence other people more than their views affect him, is naturally anxious to play a big, brave part in life. Putting aside the merely artistic pleasure in applause and admiration, which is without doubt a strong motive in many cases, a man may well desire to wield power and influence, to be somebody, to handle large interests successfully, to have his hand on the machine of politics or commerce or society. Such an ambition is not necessarily a mean one, though this depends upon whether a man looks to the doing of great work in a great way, or to the rewards and emoluments of such work. Probably *monstrari digito*, as

---

* It may roughly be said that the professions which stand highest in the social scale are the army, the navy, the bar, land agency, and the civil service. We may perhaps include with these artists, architects and literary men. In the second rank comes the solicitor, the engineer, the doctor, the schoolmaster; the Church, which formerly belonged to the upper grade, now stands somewhat apart, and may be called a vocation rather than a profession.

1

Horace said, is a powerful motive with the young; it seems an admirable thing to be received with deference, courteously treated, obeyed, reverenced; though the man who has attained to a position which commands respect often finds the publicity tiresome and the deference conventional. Still, few successful men would view with equanimity the possibility of eclipse and obscurity; and it would be foolish to pretend that power and influence and position are not some of the best and most pleasant things that the world has to give; indeed, in spite of the warnings of uneasy moralists, it is clear that they often have a very beneficial effect upon a character.

But the man who adopts the profession of a schoolmaster cannot hope for these things in any great measure. If he takes orders he may aspire to a headmastership, and then, at a time of life when the spirits begin to flag a little, and when the physical alertness that is so essential a feature in dealing with the young is a little dimmed, he can hope for a more mature sphere of action in a parish, a canonry, or even a bishopric. But the average lay schoolmaster is practically debarred from a later career. He must make up his mind that his activities will probably begin and end with his mastership. Then, too – for it is as well to state the disadvantages frankly and candidly – he must look forward to doing a good deal of drudgery of various kinds. He must be prepared to go on insisting on a relentless accuracy, to continue correcting the same mistakes year after year, to impose upon tender minds a number of facts which are not superficially attractive, and which possibly he may have the misfortune to consider unimportant in themselves. He must be prepared for an almost inevitable intellectual cramping of interests, prepared to deal incessantly with minds in which he can take nothing for granted, which have neither knowledge nor necessarily interest. He must perpetually resist the impulse to soar, and must return again and again to elementary facts and simple problems in their most unrefreshing stage; to be an interesting teacher he must have a mind resembling a number of *Tit-Bits*, stored with superficial knowledge arranged in an attractive form.

Then if he aspires to keep a boarding-house, he must be prepared to face humble domestic problems, which tend too to grow most complicated every year, in the spirit of a caterer or hotel manager. No enthusiasm will ever quite succeed in gilding a trade which consists, in part, of providing food and lodging for a large number of people and charging them rather more than they cost.

Then, too, in his dealings with men of equal age, he must be prepared to be considered rather a tiresome person, living somewhat apart from the main current of affairs. He must be prepared to meet people who will be on the look-out for any signs of a dictatorial manner, and quick to mark any tendency towards a lust for imparting information. And he must be prepared also to be treated as a kind of clergyman, as a man who is bound by his profession to adopt a conventional view and to luxuriate in genial priggishness.

He cannot hope to accumulate great wealth, unless indeed he is in the position of having sufficient capital to start a private school of his own; and even then he runs a certain risk of failure, unless his aptitude for leadership is instinctive and his connections secure.

These are the superficial disadvantages of the trade; and it must be confessed that they are considerable.

The superficial advantages are soon stated. A mastership in a good public school – and it is the holders of such posts for whose consideration these pages are intended – means an immediate competence. It means a life of regular work, with possibilities of physical exercise tending on the whole to health and activity; it means a prospect of marriage; it means good holidays; and it means also the interest which always attaches to dealing with human beings at a lovable and interesting age; it means a succession and an increasing circle of friends; and it implies, which is not the least of advantages, a connection with an institution which calls out feelings of patriotism, affection, and pride, an institution with traditions and hopes, with a past, a vivid present, and a great future.

We may now shortly consider the question of a vocation, and I am afraid that it must be confessed that the profession of a schoolmaster is one that is more apt to be entered by those who have no particular vocation for anything else, than any other profession. A certain number of young men go up to the University every year who are conscious that they will be obliged to earn their living, without any very definite idea as to how it is to be done. Of these some become civil servants, some solicitors, some drift into literature, some become University dons, some go into business, but many tend to become schoolmasters; to be a doctor, an engineer, a clergyman, or a soldier, it is necessary to make up the mind at the outset of the University career. But it may be said that while there are some few who by traditions or predilection are destined to be schoolmasters, a far larger number have a vague feeling at the back of their minds that if everything else fail they can always be teachers. Putting this latter class aside for a moment, even of the former class there are comparatively few who look forward with eagerness or enthusiasm to the profession: a large proportion think dimly of teaching as a profession which they would not actively dislike. They have seen it practised more or less successfully by the masters whom they had been under; and it may be said roughly that schoolmasters are probably the only professional men whom the boys have seen at close quarters for a considerable time engaged in their professional work. At home, if they have lived in a professional circle, they have generally seen the domestic side of the practitioners among whom they have lived, they have seen them, in fact, off duty; but schoolmasters they have seen, for several impressible years, on duty; and if the spectacle does not produce any very lively enthusiasm – the spectacle of schoolmastering as it is generally practised in England – at all events it is something to say that it does not nowadays breed a very active dislike. The life of the schoolmaster does not appear wholly unattractive; the possibility of a continuity of physical exercise is probably one of its main charms to young men; but in other respects the life appears tolerable. There is a certain attractiveness about the perpetual exercise of minute control; there is a sense, very strong in the British character, of pleasure in exercising discipline and showing power, even in a limited circle. And there is, moreover, a growing tendency to look upon the public school master as on the whole a worthy, good-humoured, and sensible man – a figure which, if it does not kindle high enthusiasm, at any rate does not present any specially sordid or repulsive features.

It must be remembered that only a small percentage of people enter professions with a very definite sense of enthusiasm for the discharge of its duties. Most people would rather look forward to a prospect of doing what they like. If the prospect of a life of absolute indolence appeals to but few, most people think that they could organise a life of leisure in a virtuous and pleasurable way. The question is whether schoolmastering is a life where the sense of vocation can be developed in the exercise of the profession itself. The answer is strongly in the affirmative.

Until recently there were a large number of men who entered the clerical profession without any strong sense of vocation. So long as they were not inconveniently sceptical, it seemed a life which resembled on a small scale and with a few disadvantages the life of a country gentleman. Many a man who took orders did so because the position was one which implied no great strain; which afforded possibilities of sport and quiet society and agricultural occupation. Such men had no burning desire to save souls or to supply the water of life to thirsting parishioners. In many cases they were aware that the parishioners to whom they intended to minister had no more desire for spiritual sustenance than they had for imparting it. But such men often turned out admirable clergymen. They were honest, kind, straightforward, virtuous; and they found moreover that any profession which brings a man into close relations with men and women is apt to soften and deepen the heart. The sight of poverty and suffering and death has a wonderful effect upon the human spirit, and such men often gained, as life went on, a pastoral if not an apostolic character. The very words of the liturgy, that meant but little to them at the beginning of their career, became charged with tender meanings and holy associations.

So it is with schoolmastering. There is no profession which is so apt, if exercised faithfully and sympathetically and tenderly, to broaden the character and enlarge the spirit. A man who goes to be a schoolmaster with the expectation of having to discharge prescribed duties and afterwards to fill his leisure time as cheerfully as he may, suddenly wakes up to find himself in the grip of all kinds of problems; he finds himself bound, like Gulliver, with all kinds of Lilliputian chains. The little people, who seem at first sight, to be all so much alike in tastes and

character, he realises are human beings with hearts and
idiosyncrasies. He finds himself guiding and leading. The
paternal, the protective instinct, which lies at the bottom of so
many male hearts, wakes up; the man who began as the
careless, self-regarding practitioner of a not very dignified
trade, discovers that he is in the thick of a very real and vivid
life, which stirs all sorts of interests and emotions and brings
home to him some of the deep realities of life.

# II

# TRAINING OF TEACHERS

I confess that I am somewhat sceptical about the training of teachers; it seems to me like training people to become good conversationalists. The receipt is to know the subject you are teaching, and to have a lively, genial, and effective personality. It seems to me that it is an art which cannot be learnt by demonstration. To train a man to teach, without confronting him with a class of his own, in stern isolation, with no one to assist him in a crisis, with no authority but his own to fall back upon, is like teaching a man to swim upon dry land. Even a profound knowledge of the subject is comparatively unimportant except in advanced work; a brisk, idle man with a knack of exposition and the art of clear statement can be a scandalously effective teacher. In fact, the more profound the knowledge of the teacher is, the more risk there is of his being unable to sympathise with the difficulties of boys, and of his being incapable of conceiving the possible depths of their ignorance. The perfect combination is sound knowledge, endless patience, and inexhaustible sympathy. A man who can keep the boys interested and amused, who can appreciate the slender nuances which differentiate the work of a boy who has tried to learn his lesson from the work of a boy who has just done enough to pass muster, will have a much greater effect on a class than a man whose knowledge is far deeper, but who has not the art of commanding attention, or of sympathising with the unformed mind. The real difficulty is the question of discipline, and no one can possibly be an effective teacher who has to be always looking about for signs of inattention and misbehaviour. And here lies the root of the matter. A man may have conducted classes satisfactorily at a training college where the disciplinary difficulty is non-existent, he may have seen and heard a lesson brilliantly conducted by an effective teacher, but when he is face to face with a class of his own, he may find that he has no real control, and that he cannot command the attention of the boys sufficiently to allow him to imitate the method he has seen successfully pursued. Moreover, in teaching, which is above all things a spontaneous, a dramatic process, the method of conducting a lesson must be to a great extent a matter of idiosyncrasy. No one can form himself upon a model. Some masters have the art of rapid questioning, some the art of exposition, and it matters little which is employed, so long as the result is alertness and interest in the boys. The best training of all would be to be able to observe through a loophole the conducting by a first-rate teacher – I say through a loophole, because there are many first-rate teachers the edge of whose teaching would be dulled if the lesson had to be conducted in the presence of a critical observer. I have myself known a master whose teaching greatly impressed the headmaster whenever he visited the schoolroom. The teacher in question was learned, accurate, and clear-headed; his questions were to the point, his explanations lucid; but the headmaster did not know that it was only his own presence that kept the class in a submissive frame of mind, and that on ordinary occasions the time of the master was so fully occupied by an entirely unsuccessful attempt to keep the boys in order that he never had an opportunity of indulging in the lucid exposition of the lesson which had seemed so impressive.

The fact is that the boys who have been through a public school themselves have practically been trained as teachers as far as training can be given. They have seen innumerable lessons given, and they can to a certain extent discriminate methods.

The teacher's aim is, after all, to make the boys think – to put them into such a frame of mind that they will take in and assimilate knowledge and make it their own, not to drive facts in like a row of nails. The best teacher I have ever heard is one who deals very little with questions, but lectures with a zest and with a certain air of bringing out facts of incredible importance, which could not be obtained in any other place and in any other circumstances. The result is that the boys are kept in state of pleased expectancy. And this knowledge is not only such as stands the test of examinations; it attracts the boys to the subject, it makes them enthusiastic.

I do not say that it is not an advantage to a man to have passed through a certain period of training, but I do maintain that such training can never make a man an effective teacher. It may just give him an inkling of how to set to work; but a sensible man, with a gift for discipline, who can realise that the small boys, whom he will almost certainly have to begin by teaching, are sure to be almost entirely ignorant and very slow of comprehension, but that if their interest can once be aroused they will make rapid progress; such a man will learn more in a week from teaching a division of his own, where he has no one to depend on but himself, than in months spent at a training college.

What I believe would be a still better system would be to attach a young master on first going to a public school, to some competent senior – to get the senior master to be present when he takes a lesson, and occasionally to take a lesson before him. But as far as mere methods are concerned, I am sure I could tell a young man in half an hour the simple dodges which have proved in my own case useful and effective.

The best training that a teacher can get is the training that he can give himself. If he has found an illustration or a story effective, let him note it down for future use; let him read widely rather than profoundly, so that he has a large stock-in-trade of anecdote and illustration. Let him try experiments; let him grasp that monotony is the one thing that alienates the attention of boys sooner than anything else; let him contrive to get brisk periods of intense work rather than long tracts of dreary work. These are facts which can only be learnt by practice and among the boys. I declare I believe that one of the most useful qualities that I have found myself to possess from the point of view of teaching is the capacity for being rapidly and easily bored myself. If the tedium of a long and dull lesson is unsupportable to myself, I have enough imagination to know that it must far worse for the boys.

Education is not and cannot be a wholly scientific thing. It is the contact of one mind with another, and it is governed by the same laws that the intercourse of men in ordinary life is governed by. A teacher must keep himself fresh in mind and body alike, and a dreary, tired, and dispirited man is not likely to produce any profound impression on the tender mind, except that the subjects which he endeavours to instil are in themselves a tedious and uninspiring business.

One last mistake I may touch upon here. I have known very worthy teachers who have insisted with conscientious perseverance in only imparting knowledge of a kind that ought to interest the well-regulated mind. Now very few minds are well-regulated, and I have found myself that the only way to interest boys is to treat frankly of what has interested myself, without any reference as to whether it ought to have interested me. The result is not invariably successful – a man must have sufficient tact to see that a hobby of his own is not always attractive to immature minds – but it is generally so; whereas to regulate one's teaching by a standard of dignity is generally to succeed in depriving it of the last shred of interest. One must be sincere in teaching above all things, and it is impossible to be convincing if one if perpetually endeavouring to enforce things in which one does not believe.

Lastly, I am inclined to think that the best system of all, if it were feasible, would be to send a young man for a few weeks to a training college *after* he has had say a year's experience of teaching in a school. He will have learnt by that time what his weak points are, he will have some idea of what the difficulties are. He will be alert to see how to deal with a lesson, how to explain, what kind of questions to put and how to put them. He will probably have acquired some enthusiasm for his art; he will realise that what seemed so simple in the hands of a skilled teacher, before he had any experience of difficulties, is not an easy matter at all.

# III

# DISCIPLINE

The power of maintaining discipline is the *unum necessarium* for a teacher; if he has not got it and cannot acquire it, he had better sweep a crossing. It insults the soul, it is destructive of all self-respect and dignity to be incessantly at the mercy of the boys. They are merciless, and the pathos of the situation never touches them at all. A friend told me the other day that at a certain public school, a division of which he was a member was often taken by a worthy man and a good scholar who was utterly incapable of preserving even a semblance of order. The conversation was general, books were flying across the room, the whole division used to rise to their feet every time the clock struck and make for the door with an air of blithe unconsciousness; he had seen the master leave his seat too and hurry to the door to put his back against it. Some of the boys – in no priggish spirit, he said, but with the feeling that the spectacle was an unworthy one – resolved among themselves to try and stop this; they waited outside the room and implored everyone to behave themselves; but it was impossible to resist the impulse, and five minutes after the lesson had begun the boy who had been most urgent in his entreaties was busily employed in constructing a long rope of quill pens, which he pushed, as a sweep pushes his jointed brush, across the room to his friends opposite.

A boy, under similar circumstances, was sent to his tutor by the master of his school division, with a complaint of serious insubordination. Little by little the story came out, and it appeared that he had put a dormouse down the master's back, between his neck and his collar, as he sat correcting an exercise. "How was I to know he drew the line at a dormouse?" said the boy tearfully, giving a dreadful glimpse of what had been tolerated.

Such stories are not edifying, but they are true; and any young teacher must take into account the fact that such things may befall himself. On the other hand, it is equally true that many masters begin badly and improve in this respect; they fight with beasts at Ephesus, and prevail. It is not easy to restore order to a division which has got thoroughly out of hand; but time passes, and a master finds a new division under him, and he has learnt experience. I think that in this respect English boys are probably different from others; they are highly independent, but on the other hand they are amenable to strict discipline, do not dislike being dragooned, and have considerable admiration for severity. They are moreover highly imitative, and if a master can by any means reduce the leading spirits to obedience, the rest will follow suit. Moreover, if a master once gets a reputation for strictness his difficulties are at an end. The boys will come to him expecting to obey, and it will never occur to them to do otherwise.

The qualities which command obedience are not easy to define. Personal impressiveness smooths the way, of course. A man must know exactly what he wants, and must go on until he gets it. It is not enough to be merely strict, a man must be good-humoured. A turn for ready repartee is a very useful thing, because a boy above all things dislikes being made to feel a fool before others. A certain quiet irony, as long as it is not cruel, is a very effective weapon, but not to be used except by indubitably good-natured men. Another very useful quality is the power of losing one's temper with dignity; almost all people, whether boys or men, dislike being confronted with anger; but it must be kept in the background. I remember a very effective master whose temper was quick, but who had it entirely under control. I do not think I ever saw him break out, but there was something singularly impressive, if anything occurred which he disliked, in a momentary silence which followed, as he sat with compressed lips and clouded brow – it made the boys feel that there was something behind which had better not be provoked. As a rule, a disciplinary difficulty had better not be dealt with on the spot; if a boy is told to wait afterwards, he has to pass a disagreeable period, wondering what is going to happen; and the excitement has a way of oozing out of the heels of the boots on such occasions. Moreover, boys are generally reasonable enough alone; there is a kind of excitement, which might be called *comitialis*, which sustains a boy in the presence of his fellows.

But the qualities of which I have spoken are mainly negative qualities, to be kept in the background as far as possible. Courtesy, approbation, appreciation are far more valuable allies; a ready smile, an agreeable manner, a rebuke given in the form of a compliment are infinitely more effective. One of the best disciplinarians I have ever seen put an end to what tended to be a disagreeable scene by saying to an ill-conditioned boy who had lost his temper, in a voice of unruffled suavity, "Smith, I don't think we see you at your best on this occasion."

It must be borne in mind that the disciplinary difficulty is greatly diminished of late years, mainly, I think, by the human and pleasant relations which begin at the private schools. A master is not necessarily yet considered as a guide, philosopher, or friend, but he is certainly no longer looked upon as a boy's natural enemy.

I am no believer in punishments; indeed, I think that to set punishments is merely a sign of weakness. Small punishments are simply irritating, and it is far better to give several warnings and then come down with all your might. Only deliberate offences deserve punishments. As to corporal punishment, the doubtful privilege of dispensing it is, at my own school, not conceded to the assistant-masters. I can only say that I have hardly ever known a case where it was required, and on the few occasions when I should have liked to cane a boy, I have never regretted that I was unable to do so. It cannot be entirely abolished, I suppose. There are a few mischievous, tiresome, malevolent boys, probably undeveloped, who require it, but even then it is better to leave it entirely in the hands of the headmaster.

My own practice is to give every new division a little pastoral lecture at the beginning of the half. To say exactly what I mean to have and exactly what I do not mean to have. To tell the boys frankly that I mean to do my best, and that I expect their best. To say that even if I cannot always praise every good piece of work, I shall not be found lacking in appreciation of it; to say that I don't deal in punishments, but that if they are necessary, they will be of a kind that will be remembered; and finally, to say that we all start as friends, and that I hope we shall remain so.

It is certainly a mistake to deal in sentiment too much – in matters of discipline the boys should have plain and common-sense motives put before them. One of the most ineffective masters I have ever known told a colleague that he had one form of appeal which he employed with invariable success. "I point," he said, "my finger at the offender, and ask him how he would like his mother to see him at the moment behaving as he is behaving." Fortunately most masters have some sense of humour which would save them from such a display of fatuity. But the difficulty that besets all schoolmasters in this particular matter is the absence of criticism. Many masters use far too much discipline and think they cannot get on without it. I have known men who are quite capable of commanding ready obedience talk of their 'tariff' of punishments; on the other hand, some men are not strict enough, and are quite content as long as there is no overt disturbance. A master ought to consider a boy who nods in a corner or a boy who pulls out his watch as a severe critic of his magisterial powers.

There is another kind of discipline about which a word may be said, which is the discipline of a house. It should follow the same lines as the discipline of a division; there should be as few rules as possible, and they should be implicitly obeyed. But in a house a master should, I believe, drop the magisterial relation as far as possible, and adopt the paternal. He should be easy, friendly, conversational. No boy should ever be surprised to see him in the house, and yet his presence there should be obviously accounted for by sociable tastes and not by a desire to be vigilant. As much authority as possible should be delegated to the upper boys, but at the same time they should not be allowed to use corporal punishment without consulting the tutor. At one time I used to think that corporal punishment of any kind should be forbidden, but I recollect an occasion when a highly conscientious captain came to tell me that he had caned three boys in the course of the evening for making a disturbance. "I know you don't like it," he said, "but what am I to do? I come up and tell them to stop, and the moment I am out of sight they begin again. I can't go and say that I shall tell you, and I must do something." Since that time I have acquiesced in its occasional use, but insist that I shall always be acquainted with it, if possible, beforehand.

Boys are highly reasonable, and if one says to a captain that after all the housemaster is ultimately held responsible, and if there were any complaint made by a boy of excessive severity, the housemaster would have to bear the blame, he has no difficulty in understanding the position.

# IV

# TEACHING

As regards the art of teaching, it is difficult to lay down rules, because every man must find out his own method. It is easy to say that the first requisite is patience, but the statement requires considerable modification. A master must, of course, realise that a great many things are perfectly clear to him which are not at all clear to the boys, but it is easy for a man of tranquil temperament to drift into a kind of indulgent easiness, which ends in the boys making no effort whatever to overcome difficulties for themselves. If a master accepts the statement too readily, "I could not make it out," and considers that a list of words written out is ample evidence of the preparation of a lesson, there are a great many boys who will prepare a list of likely-looking words and take no further trouble about a lesson. It is much better for a master to insist briskly that some kind of sense should be made, though he must tactfully discriminate between the industrious, muddled boy and the boy who is simply indolent.

Then, too, teaching should be crisp and clear and decided. The greatest compliment ever paid to a teacher by a dull boy was when the latter said that the books muddled him, because Hermann said that a passage meant one thing, and Schneidewin said that it meant another, but that So-and-so told you what it really did mean.

I have known of excellent scholars who deprived their teaching of much of its value by being too tentative, or even by having recourse to a dictionary in public. It is better to be perfectly decisive, even if you may be occasionally wrong. This principle would not, of course, apply to older or abler boys, nor would it apply to private tuition with a smaller class. But for boys of small capacity it is necessary, by some means or other, to disabuse them of a not unnatural delusion, much encouraged by commentators, that writer in a foreign language might have meant anything, and may be made to mean anything, by juggling with words. It is certain that many boys, under our system of education, do not understand that a writer has had a definite thought in his mind which he is expressing in a natural way; and that our difficulty in understanding it arises from an absence of complete and instinctive familiarity with the medium of expression. For such boys decisiveness is a pure gain.

Moreover, in young and sharp boys there is often a strong vein of a certain maliciousness; and if they imagine that a teacher is imperfectly acquainted with his subject, they are quite capable of expending their dexterity and energy in framing apparently innocent questions, with a view to exposing, if possible, gaps in a teacher's knowledge. With such boys decisiveness is a necessity.

A school lesson should be of the nature of a dramatic performance, from which some interest and amusement may be expected; while at the same time there must be solid and business-like work done. Variety of every kind should be attempted; the blackboard should be used, there should be some simple jesting, there should be some anecdote, some disquisition, and some allusion if possible to current events, and the result should be that the boys should not only feel that they have put away some definite knowledge under lock and key, but also that they have been in contact with a lively and more mature mind. Exactly in what proportion the cauldron should be mingled, and what its precise ingredients should be, must be left to the taste and tact of the teacher. A man must be quick to discern if the boys by apparently innocent questions can set him off in a discursive talk on things in general, and he must also be quick to see when to unbend the bow. The shield which is within the reach of every boy against the too insistent demands of a teacher is absolute inattention, combined, by practice, with a demure look and downcast eye, capable of deceiving the most alert. I believe that there is a certain commercial instinct in most boys, which leads them to like to get good value for their money; and I have heard boys complain about an interesting teacher that they never seemed to know the lesson after school was over. It is hardly necessary here to go into all the various little dodges for securing variety which will be useful to a teacher, but an instance or two may be given. The Greek irregular verbs are not a particularly refreshing form of study, but by asking the various forms in quick succession, making the boys score a mark if they get one right, and reading out the marks obtained, a certain emulation is arrived at which at all events makes a boy anxious to get as many right as he can. Again, if it is desired that boys should master a difficult thing like the Greek conditional sentence, after a lucid explanation various illustrative sentences may be dictated, supplying the Greek words to be used, and the boys required to do them then and there on paper, it being stipulated that as soon as the whole division can do them rightly you will turn to some less strenuous work, and not till then. It is rewarding to see the intense zeal which the very slowest boys will take under such circumstances to get the thing correct.

Some teachers deal largely in questions, but if the class is large it needs almost genius to keep question and answer going with sufficiently rapidity to ensure universal attention. Moreover, if the requisite enthusiasm is invoked, it requires a good deal of masterfulness to keep it within decorous bounds. I myself believe that questioning should be more used in small classes, and that with a large class a form of lecturing, interspersed with questions, is the more effective. But here again the idiosyncrasy of the man comes in; if a teacher has the gift of asking questions of a kind that stimulate curiosity by their form, and make the answering them into a brisk species of intellectual lawn-tennis, he is probably a very good teacher. But few men will probably have sufficient mental agility – and what is more, still fewer boys – and the result will be apt to be that the game will be played between the master and a few boys of some mental rapidity, and the majority of the class will have but a faint idea of what is going on.

Some masters certainly attach an extravagant value to questions and answers. It is recorded of an eminent headmaster that he insisted so strongly on a general and simultaneous response being made to his questions that the more torpid intellects used under cover of the intelligent replies of the better informed boys to shout "Borrioboola-Gha!" with an appearance of lively zeal. The system was exposed by the fact that a worthy boy, of some athletic prominence, happened to fall asleep on a summer's day, and on waking heard the headmaster's voice pause for a moment, and anxious to make up for his brief period of unconsciousness, indulged in his usual cry with a very good will. But the headmaster had asked no question and the lamentable syllables fell with appalling effect upon the quiet air. He was instantly ordered from the room for gross insubordination, and was obliged in order to save the situation to give the happy practice away.

Of course it goes without saying that the liveliest teaching is spoiled by any want of naturalness. The master should be, and should not be ashamed of showing himself to be, generally interested in what is going on, and not be merely bursting with superfluous information. To sit and be pumped into, as Carlyle said, speaking of Coleridge's conversation, is never an exhilarating process. But naturalness, like humility, is a virtue difficult of cultivation, because the absence of self-consciousness is a necessary condition of effectiveness.

One form of affectation has I believe very bad results. It is the custom of many teachers to speak as if all the authors whom they were expounding were equally valuable and equally attractive. I do not think that anything destroys the critical and appreciative faculties in boys so quickly as this. I believe myself that it is good for a teacher to have strong prejudices, just as Dr Arnold's feeling for Livy partook, as his pupils said, of an almost personal animosity. I think that a master should be ready to say frankly what his candid opinion of an author is, giving his reasons, and saying at the same time that it is purely a matter of opinion. He should not be afraid of pointing out the extraordinary and vicious coagulations to be found in Thucydides, the feeble fluencies of Ovid, the lapses from good taste in Horace, the sententiousness of Euripides; and then when he freely and generously praises a heroic passage of Homer, a pathetic line of Virgil, a piece of lively narrative by Xenophon, the ringing crispness of Horace's stanzas, his words have weight. Boys will see that there is such a thing as good style and bad style, will begin moreover, however feebly, to have preferences and to have a reason for a preference. Of course it is of little use to get the boys to take hasty opinions on trust, but if a master can get a boy into the habit of forming an opinion at all, he has done valuable work. A conscientious master may say that everyone ought to admire Virgil, and not arouse any very definite enthusiasm. But a man who has delivered a brisk diatribe against the faults of style perceptible in Thucydides on the previous day, will be heard with attention and respect if he says of Virgil that he is accepted as one of the great writers of the earth, and that if anyone finds that he can see nothing to admire or love in Virgil, it is probably he and not Virgil that needs to be changed.

"Like it, or dislike it," said a vigorous teacher once to a class of boys in my presence, "it doesn't matter twopence which you do; only don't say that you don't *care*."

# V

# WORK

The question of work is twofold. It must be considered (1) from the point of view of the boy; (2) from the point of view of the master.

(1) I believe very strongly in giving boys plain and sensible reasons for the work that is required of them. Idleness is not a vice of little boys as a rule. They have not begun to question the usefulness of particular kinds of work, and they do not dislike occupation. If they are disposed to neglect their work, it will be generally found that there is some strong counter-attraction; and thus, among young boys, idleness is more likely to occur with boys of a certain ability, with natural tastes of some kind to which they sacrifice routine work. Therefore with small boys, when idleness occurs, it is better to make work simply a matter of obedience. But as boys get older and begin to question the usefulness of certain kinds of work, I have found it wise to tell them plainly that every boy cannot be interested in all the work that he does, but that every boy ought to be interested in doing his plain duty. It can be pointed out that they will probably have work to do in the world, and that the work will probably be to a great extent uninteresting, and that it is advisable for everyone to cultivate the habit of doing well and conscientiously whatever is demanded of him. It is as well, I think, to say to a boy that this is the reason why honest work is expected of him, and that this is a good reason for doing it; but that if it is not a sufficient reason, it will be necessary to fall back on the simple though not so intelligent reason, that it is at all events a master's business to require it. A master ought, moreover, to spare the boys as far as possible all unnecessary

trouble, and to say that he intends to do so, and that he expects in return that the boys will do conscientiously whatever common sense demands. I can only say that I have found these reasons appreciated by boys and the results satisfactory.

On the other hand a good many boys are not at all averse to real mental effort; and a master's business is to try and see that there *is* mental effort, and not to be contented with mere mechanical copying.

One detail which may be mentioned here is the question of repetition lessons. It presents a great difficulty – because it is work which gives little trouble to some boys who have a good verbal memory, and is an infinite and weary labour to others. I am inclined to think that classical repetition lessons are a mistake except for boys of definite classical ability; if they are an inevitable part of the curriculum, then the trouble should be lightened as far as possible by allowing slower boys to say their lesson from a written translation; but better still, I think, is the use of English poetry, which develops the memory easily. Very few boys dislike learning English, and it is a great advantage to give boys a good repertory of English poetry. The classical repetition lessons do not remain in the mind, and thus do not, I think, justify the reason which is often given for their retention – that the practice increases a boy's vocabulary.

(2) Then comes the question of the work from the master's point of view. There is a wise saying that nine-tenths of the noble work done in the world is drudgery, which is often misused as if it meant that nine-tenths of the drudgery done in the world is noble work. This has no semblance of truth in it. It is of course a question for headmasters, but I believe myself that the absolute drudgery inseparable from teaching should be reduced to a minimum. Indeed I will go further and say that I believe that it is the positive duty of a master to save himself as

far as possible from unnecessary drudgery.

Of course the principle could be used sophistically, but I am writing for conscientious men, and I believe that there is a great deal of Pharisaism in the matter. I have known masters who have so immersed themselves in the laborious correction of exercises that they have not only lost all freshness of mind and spirit, but have sacrificed all possibility of reading and enlarging their own minds to a kind of dull self-satisfaction in the amount of hours spent over correction of exercises which really was of no benefit to the boys.

The boy must of course have his mistakes pointed out to him, he must feel that his work is vigilantly reviewed; but the moment that a master, from a sense of duty, luxuriates in corrections which do not benefit the boy, that moment the master is ceasing to do his duty. Of course one does not mean that a master should gain time for amusement or physical exercise by neglecting his duty. But no system which tends to bring a master in mountains of unproductive work is a good system.

For instance, it is the way in many schools to let the boys do a written exercise in school, for the master to take it away, and then perhaps some days after to return the exercise underlined and to go through it. Now this is deliberately sacrificing one of the most active intellectual processes of the boyish mind. Almost all boys who have been doing a piece of work, say Latin prose or translation, have a kind of anxiety at the time as to what their mistakes have been, how the passage should be turned, and so forth. While the thing is hot in their minds they would really like to know how it should be done; but the lapse of a few hours entirely chills their interest and obliterates their memory of what they have found difficult.

I believe that a few minutes should always be spent at the end of such a lesson by the master in going through the piece and requiring the boys as far as possible to understand their own mistakes. He should even say that the mark a boy gets will depend to a certain extent upon how far they have detected their own mistakes. Then he should review the exercise, if possible, with the boy beside him. It is not a gain of time upon the other system, but it is immensely more valuable, and a master moreover who cares about his art has the knowledge that the boys are personally interested in the work – and one never grudges time spent in work where the boy is actively interested; what one does grudge is the work which is weariness to the master and unprofitable for the boy.

Of course there must be drudgery, and the drudgery is bound to be great. Many masters know that a little bit of writing work is of infinite relief in the middle of a construing lesson; to have a few lines written out by the boys is like requiring all of them to construe a passage, but a hard-worked master will often avoid it because of the labour involved in looking over the passage afterwards. My own belief is that such a passage need only be cursorily inspected, just to see that no boy has shirked the task. And I believe that we should be content to do a good deal more written work in this rough way, and that we should find the results very valuable.

The other practice, that of being obliged to scrutinise all the boys' written work with minute care, is, I believe, a survival from the time when the boys in public schools did one or two written exercises in a week, which were made as perfect as possible; and I believe that still one exercise should be treated in that way, in as literary a fashion as possible, to give boys what Dr Hawtrey used to call 'the sweet pride of authorship', but that a great deal more should be done roughly and easily.

A very great headmaster, who produced more good scholars than, perhaps, any other teacher, used, I believe, to be singularly careless in looking over his exercises. Huge bundles used to accumulate on his study table; he would send for a boy, take out an exercise at random, and give him half an hour of splendid teaching. Many exercises were not looked over at all, but the boy had had the practice in doing them, whereas if the headmaster had felt obliged to scrutinise every exercise conscientiously he could only have given the boy a minute or two at the most of rapid indication of mistakes.

After all, the improvement of the mental capacity of the boys is the object, an object which many conscientious teachers are apt to forget in the dreary satisfaction of performing mechanical duties, as they would say, 'in the great Taskmaster's eye'.

Again, I am a great believer in the value of note-taking for boys. It helps them to see the point, to record it rapidly, and moreover it acts as a little anchor to the restless mind, which otherwise voyages about in very different waters; and finally it just relieves that slight physical restlessness which is apt to beset boys when sitting for an hour or so without anything particular to do but to listen. Yet many masters are deterred from encouraging the practice simply because of the enormous toil it imposes upon them if they make any attempt to look over the notes. But it is quite possible to take a few note-books at a time, dip for specimens, and write a little criticism of an encouraging nature, if possible, for the boys' satisfaction. Moreover, it is much more interesting work than most exercises, because the master really gets a peep into a boy's mind.

The conclusion is that it is not a self-indulgence, but a plain duty, for masters to keep themselves fresh and active-minded; and the spirit in which a man allows himself to be carried helplessly down in a stream of mechanical duties is not only not praiseworthy, but highly reprehensible.

# VI

# INTELLECT

It must be frankly admitted that the intellectual standard maintained at the English public schools is low; and what is more serious, I do not see any evidence that it is tending to become higher. The subject of athletics will be treated separately, but I will here say that I have no desire to attack the system of organised athletics. Indeed, the system has great and obvious merits; but what I plead for is the coordination of interests. I honestly believe that the masters of public schools have two strong ambitions – to make the boys good and to make them healthy; but I do not think that they care about making them intellectual; intellectual life is left to take care of itself. My belief is that a great many masters look upon the boys' work as a question of duty – that is, they consider it from the moral standpoint, and not from the intellectual. Of course, the public schools must reflect to a certain extent the tendencies of the nation; and the nation is certainly not preoccupied with intellectual interests. The nation appears to me to be mainly preoccupied with two ambitions: success, which in many cases is identical with wealth; and manly conduct, which is a combination of aptitude for outdoor exercises with the practice of wholesome virtues. To put it in academical terms, the national ideal seems to be a mixture of the Hebraistic and the Spartan systems – national prosperity, with a certain standard of right conduct, and physical prowess. It seems to me that the Athenian ideal – that of strong intellectual capacity – is left out of sight altogether. I do not deny that right conduct, national prosperity and physical well-being are great conveniences, but I do not see why intellectual strength should not take its place

29

side by side with the others; and if anywhere, it is in the public schools of the country that the standard ought to be maintained. I believe that we have condescended far too much to the boy's ideal of life. The boy's ideal is to be successful and to be strong, and accordingly that is what he is primarily encouraged to be, so long as he is virtuous.

So far removed is the intellectual ideal from the mind of the ordinary man that it is difficult even to write of it without being misunderstood. It is understood to be a kind of mixture of priggishness and pedantry; it is confused with learning; it is supposed that the intellectual man is the kind of man who always wants to talk about books. The current view about intellectual powers was admirably summed up by a friend of mine, who said, speaking of a clever woman, "What I like about her is that though she is such a clever woman, she does not allow it to make her disagreeable." The truth is that where an atmosphere is not intellectual, it needs a certain priggishness, or a certain consciousness of high aim and worth, to talk resolutely on subjects in which others are frankly not interested.

The aim ought not to be to turn everyone into a literary personage. Literature is only one province of the intellectual life. But what should be aimed at is that people should have interests, views, subjects; that indoor life should not be a series of tedious hours to be beguiled with billiards or bridge, or with anticipations or recollections of open-air amusements. My idea of an intellectual person is one whose mind is alive to ideas; who is interested in politics, religion, science, history, literature; who knows enough to wish to know more, and to listen if he cannot talk; a person who is not at the mercy of a new book, a leading article, or the chatter of an irresponsible outsider; a person who is not insular, provincial, narrow-minded, contemptuous.

My own belief is that a good many young boys have the germ

of intellectual life in them, but that in many cases it dies a natural death from mere inanition. They find themselves in a society like a public school, where their path in life is clearly indicated and where public feeling is very urgent and very precise. They find that they have a good deal of work to do, to which no particular intellectual interest attaches. Out of school there are games and talk about games; and unless a boy is very keenly interested in intellectual things, his interest is not likely to survive in an atmosphere which is all alive, indeed, but where intellectual things are, to put it frankly, unfashionable. If his home is one where intellect is valued, he has a fair chance of keeping interest up in a timid and secluded way.

The question of how to alter this is a difficult one. It can hardly be done by definite organisations such as societies, because the boys have already so many engagements that a new one is apt to degenerate into a bore. Good lectures can do a little; a good library can do a little; but, so far as schools can influence national tendency at all, I believe that the only way is for the masters to be interested themselves. If a man is really alive to what is going on, if he reads the papers, if he reads books, if he uses his holidays wisely in travel, reading, and the society of interesting people, it is impossible that the boys who come under his influence, considering how extraordinarily imitative boys are, should not be affected by this in some degree.

I remember well being decidedly influenced as a boy by a man of the kind that I have described. He had a certain magnetic gift, I imagine; but his allusions to literature and history seemed to open doors into all sorts of roomy and spacious corridors. It used to seem to me, and it was so with others, that he lived habitually in a world that was bigger, brighter, more entertaining than the ordinary world. The man was no prig – he never hinted contempt for people who did not care about his own subjects; he merely brought, like the wise householder, out of his treasure things new and old; and many boys felt that they would like to have similar treasures in the background too.

Therefore I maintain that it is not an advisable thing so much as a positive duty for teachers to contrive some intellectual life for themselves; to live in the company of good books and big ideas. Everyone cannot be interested in everything, but everyone is capable of being interested in something; and I do not very much care what the subject is provided only that there is a little glow, a little enthusiasm about it.

Let me mention a little educational experiment which I have tried with considerable effect, both as evidence that the intellectual interest is stronger than is often imagined, and also that it is possible to stimulate it without travelling beyond the bounds of normal work. I have added, as a rule, to a written exercise called History Questions a voluntary question connected with the history we are doing in school. I have taken, for instance, the conspiracy of Catiline, and I have told any boys who care to attempt it, to treat it exactly as they like – as a letter from a conspirator describing a meeting, as a fragment from a narrative poem, as a dramatic scene – whatever they prefer. The result has been that in a very normal class of thirty boys I have found week after week some eight or ten of these answers attempted. One boy has treated it comically (not always humorously) in the style of the Bab Ballads; another has written a fragment of a play; another has attempted a passage in the style of Sir Walter Scott; another has written a letter; others have attempted to describe the scene of a meeting of conspirators in the style of Harrison Ainsworth. I contrive to read these attempts through with the boys, criticise them seriously, make respectful suggestions; and I have no sort of doubt that they are keenly interested in and think more of this than perhaps of any other school exercise. It leads to no neglect of work; but neither is it only the successful workers who are the best performers. My best lyrical poet once was a boy who could scarcely get through a piece of Latin prose without a huge crop of blunders, but who wrote flowing and spirited English lyrics with lively satisfaction. It is ridiculous to pretend that this is not good for the boys; it only shows how starved a curriculum it is that does not provide some pabulum for the literary interest that is latent in far more minds than is generally supposed.

The classicists who argue strenuously for the retention of Greek in schools use as one of their strongest claims that the Greek is so august a literature. I agree, with reservations. But I also maintain that a very small percentage of the boys who do Greek ever get within measurable distance of appreciating it as literature, and that yet among those very boys there are many who are capable of appreciating style and treatment in their own language. I am not a great advocate of using English literature in school for text-books. The treatment of literature by commentators is, as a rule, so profoundly unintelligent that I should be sorry to see it reduced to a subject. Neither do I at all desire that intellectual stimulus should be the only thing aimed at. It tends to make a mind loose, flabby, and dilettante. The mind should be exercised on work which requires grip and assiduity, but deliberately to omit intellectual enjoyment from our programme, to pass over one of the strongest of boyish faculties, seems to me the kind of mistake that will be regarded some years hence as both pitiable and ludicrous. We should never expect a boy to become a good player at any game unless he enjoyed it, and how we dare to exclude enjoyment so rigorously from our system of education is one of those mysteries that is difficult to fathom. The result is that we send out from our public schools year after year many boys who hate knowledge and think books dreary, who are perfectly self-satisfied and entirely ignorant, and, what is worse, not ignorant in a wholesome and humble manner, but arrogantly and contemptuously ignorant – not only satisfied to be so, but thinking it ridiculous and almost unmanly that a young man should be anything else.

# VII

# ORIGINALITY

It has been said that the public school system is built upon conventions, and that it is a foe to all originality. I must respectfully claim to disagree. Such originality as is extinguished by conventions is not of a very high order. The only originality that is worth having is that of the mind and heart, and I doubt whether that is ever extinguished by superficial conventionalities. I agree that the public school tends to develop a certain type of character, but it is a type above the average, and I believe it raises more characters to its level than it depresses characters down to it. Public opinion in schools is apt to be very tyrannical in small details such as dress and deportment, and this, I think, is a distinct advantage, because the standard it demands of dress is decent, and of deportment is manly. And no one is the worse, however original his mind may be, for dressing and behaving like a gentleman. Anyone whose originality is confined to eccentricity in dress and demeanour is simply a foolish *poseur*, and I should look upon the public school standard in this respect as an excellent discipline. In such matters conventionality is a mere relief, because questions of dress and deportment become simply mechanical and habitual, and leave the mind free to concern itself with other matters.

The question whether athletics, as practised at public schools, have a cramping effect on development will be considered more in detail under the head of athletics, and so I will merely say here that though athletic ambitions are temporarily apt to be rather absorbing, and tend to assume exaggerated proportions in the case of boys whose intellectual outfit is small

35

and whose minds are naturally rather narrow, I do not believe that they disturb the equilibrium of minds which are at all above the average; indeed, I would go further and say that they tend to have a wholesome effect on boys whose minds are highly developed, and, if anything, maintain the balance of physical sanity rather than destroy it. Boys whose minds are precocious or prematurely developed are apt to look upon exercise as a tiresome interference with their own pursuits, and I believe that it does distinct good in enabling them to give due weight to the necessity of keeping the body in good condition, a lesson which is apt to be taught those who slight it in early life by premature infirmities.

There remains then the question as to whether the view of intellectual and ethical things which prevails in schools has a cramping effect on the original minds that come within its influence, and I am inclined to think that it has very little, simply because it is most negative. I am not at all sure that a very strong intellectual or spiritual influence exerted upon immature minds is not in itself more cramping than none at all, because the mind is run into a certain mould at a time when impressions are very permanent, and before sufficient independence of character has been arrived at for the mind to exert its critical faculties at all. I do not think that a boy at a public school gets much sympathy in his intellectual ambition or his spiritual emotions; but I do not think it very desirable that he should, because the time has not really come for their development. Such sympathy as is useful to him should be secret and occasional rather than open and constant; and I should look with great anxiety on the future of the boys of a school who lived at high pressure intellectually and emotionally. The independence allowed to a boy of any originality is considerable, and other boys trouble themselves very little what a boy thinks of or dreams about so long as in his appearance and behaviour he shows a decent compliance with conventional things.

The question here is rather what a master's attitude should be in the matter; and here I confess that schools are rather at fault. A master must, of course, show a similarly decent compliance with conventional standards; he must be interested and express interest in games, and he must not despise the day of small things, the homely interests and events of school life, otherwise he will simply forfeit sympathy. But I think that it is a great misfortune and mistake if the boys think that a master's horizon of thought is exactly the same as their own, if they imagine that he is preoccupied with the question of who is to be in the school Eleven, or the precise nuances in the play of the school forwards.

Again, a master should be very quick to notice any originality of tastes or interests among his boys, and be ready to sympathise or help. He should be able to take an interest in what a boy reads or dreams or thinks about; he should be able to speak on occasion of spiritual things without affectation, and at the same time without embarrassment. I do not mean that any good can be done by a man pretending to have felt or thought deeply on matters in which he is indifferent, but I would contend that a professed teacher has no business to be indifferent, and that a master without some intellectual and spiritual ideal is as much out of place as a doctor without sympathy, or a clergyman who despised religion. And here comes the difficulty. A man may conscientiously take a mastership in order to teach a certain subject, if he knows his subject and is a competent disciplinarian. But I do not think that anyone has any business to enter upon tutorial relations unless he has got some definite intellectual views, and is living an intellectual life of his own; or a boarding-house, unless he has some intention of exerting influence in the right direction. I shall propose to discuss the question of religion later, but I am quite sure it is no more right to take a boarding-house for the sake of the profits and the position than it is for a clergyman to accept a living on the same grounds. Here I am convinced that some sense of vocation is an absolute necessity.

A master then who holds the position of tutor or housemaster should be carefully on the look out for signs of originality and definite bias among the boys, and do his best, like the man in the *Pilgrim's Progress*, secretly to cast oil upon the fire. He should try to see that every boy has some subject at least in which he is interested, and he should try to make it easy for every boy to pursue that subject, rather than to try to conform all his boys to the usual type, or to bring them under the subject in which he himself happens to be interested. The curriculum nowadays of a public school is a varied one, and where classics, science, history, mathematics, and modern languages are taught it is hard to say that any boy's powers are doomed to starvation. At the same time it is certain that a great many of these subjects are not taught in a stimulating way, and that a good many teachers do their duty conscientiously, but without any particular enthusiasm. Nevertheless, in a staff of masters there are sure to be enthusiasts in every branch, and a tutor should endeavour to encourage relations between his boys who are interested in the subjects and the men who are interested in them too. Of course time is the perennial difficulty. The system must be all-embracing, and my own experience of a public school master's life is that there is practically very little time when relations with boys other than those with whom some official connection exists can be cultivated at all. I believe that if a man does his work thoroughly at a public school, sees a certain amount of his colleagues socially – which is absolutely essential to general harmony – and does a little independent intellectual work of his own, the residue of time that is left is very small indeed; and this I think is an almost inevitable evil, and can only be met by those in authority resolutely diminishing all work that is unprofitable from the master's point of view. The great lack in a schoolmaster's life is time for recollection and repose. He spins along like a busy top from morning to night, and it is easy to think that if you have spun and buzzed through the hours you have done your duty in a weary way; but there is very little of the feeding in green pastures and leading forth beside the waters of comfort, and the result is that we consider our problems hastily and scantily; we consider prompt action invariably better than quiet reflection. And indeed we have most of us time to do the one and no time at all to do the other.

# VIII

# PRAISE

There is one potent educational force which is often neglected by our educators – the power of praise. As a rule, it goes against the grain in Englishmen to praise, generously and outspokenly. They call it 'paying compliments', and mix it up with insincerity. There is a foolish old proverb, which represents the surliness of grim generations of Englishmen, that 'Fine words butter no parsnips'. It is entirely untrue; just as love can give a savour to a dinner of herbs, so praise, judicious and sincere praise, can make boys contented with simple and Spartan fare. Of course, it must not be all praise; but a schoolmaster who can find fault sharply and seriously, and can at the same time praise frankly, has a great power in his hands. And I think that schoolmasters should resolutely overcome their British dislike to express appreciation. To tell a division of boys who have been working briskly and good-humouredly that they have done so, is far more likely to keep them brisk and good-humoured than to grumble at the first and natural signs of inattention. To praise diligence, to find words of appreciation for a thoughtful piece of work, is far more likely to produce further diligence than to be critical and cold.

A lady of my acquaintance once kept a party of Rural Deans happy and amused for an hour by the simple expedient of asking them what was the greatest compliment they had ever been paid. Most of the party, it is true, said that it was when their wives did them the honour to accept them, but this sacrifice paid to marital duty they expanded in easy egotism. Is it not the experience of everyone that compliments live far longer in the memory than criticism? The normal human being explains criticism away by reflecting that the critic is only imperfectly acquainted with the conditions: but with compliments one instinctively feels that the speaker has true insight into the situation.

This leads me to a very important part of the schoolmaster's duty – that of writing reports. I declare I have often been ashamed to see how these hasty and ill-considered documents are stored in family treasures, and become part of the archives of a house. I believe that the greatest possible care is well repaid in this somewhat distasteful duty. It is the schoolmaster's business to do the boy full justice, not merely to indulge in criticism. If a due proportion of credit, where credit is due, is intermingled, the arrows tipped with honey, are gratefully received. Most parents do not want elaborate details of the work. They want to be assured that the boy has tried to do his duty, they want the impression that the boy has made upon the master.

Still more important is the letter that the housemaster should write to the parents at the end of each half. I grudge no time and labour spent over this. Of course it seems tiresome to say the same kind of thing over and over again. But if the master knows the boy and cares for him, his view will insensibly alter year by year, and a master should try to put a graphic picture of the boy on paper each half. Of course this comes easier to some men than others. But I believe that the seed thus sown is apt to be very fruitful indeed. All attempts at literary smartness should be avoided, and especially all sarcasm. Parents are apt to feel such things acutely, and to resent any summary criticism of a boy. Thus a parent once wrote to a friend of mine about a report to which several masters had contributed: 'The gentleman who writes in red ink and signs himself G. F. seems to have lost his temper.' Again, a report from a master which said, 'I can teach the boy nothing', drew from an indignant parent a letter to the headmaster remonstrating with him for retaining on the staff a man 'who by his own confession is incapable of communicating the simplest knowledge to the boys'.

Parents are naturally partial, but they do not resent criticism if it is part of a sincere attempt to understand and to describe the boy. Indeed, they are often very grateful for it.

# IX

# THE BOARDING-HOUSE

It has always seemed to me that as far as possible the school should be constructed on the basis of the home, and that there should be, if possible, a home side to school life; and therefore I am inclined to think that schoolmasters should be celibates, or rather that housemasters should be, though this may appear at first sight paradoxical. It is, however, in any case, a counsel of perfection, and cannot be seriously urged, though it is only too sadly plain what havoc the suspension of the celibate rule has worked in the Universities.

The celibate housemaster has several obvious advantages. In the first place, he is free from domestic cares to a great extent; he is not obliged to regard his profession primarily as a money-making concern. Then, too, he has no domestic ties and can bestow his time and his interest wholly on his boys. The paternal instinct is strongly developed in many men who have no experience of paternity; and the married man with a wife and children is bound both by instinct and necessity to give the best of his heart to his family. Most men have only a limited capacity for affection, and if this is absorbed by the nearer domestic circle it cannot overflow among the boys.

The golden rule for the housemaster is to have unlimited affection and no sentimentality. Of course, some boys will inevitably be more interesting than others, and it is a difficult matter to proffer interest constantly to boys who reply in monosyllables, who never ask a question or originate a remark, and who are obviously bored by any relations with a master apart from official duties. But there are very few boys of this type; and I can only say that I have very seldom found a boy who is not in some way interesting if you can get on the right side of him. Most boys are interested in themselves, and very few boys can resist the charm of finding themselves interesting to another.

The root of the matter is to let a boy understand from the very first that friendship is intended and offered; and it is not enough to be vaguely friendly; it is better to tell a new boy when he comes that you desire that he will not merely look upon you as a master, but will really believe that you are a friend. This is to most new boys, coming timidly to a new place, peopled by vague ogres, an immense relief; and it is interesting to compare the change in the glance of a new boy from the time when he enters your study in the charge of a parent, and gazes with wonder and dismay at the man who is to rule his life for several years, with the glance of shy friendliness with which he meets you when you have indicated plainly that friendship is to be the basis of your relations.

After that time it is mainly a matter of idiosyncrasy; the thing is made comparatively easy at my own school, where the boys have separate rooms and where it is the custom for the housemaster to go round after prayers to see the boys until the lights are out. This is a duty I never curtail, probably because it is a pleasure, though it is a time that is apt to be chosen for meetings, and though it is sometimes a temptation to return to other work. But I attach the greatest importance to these visits. You see the boy at his best and cheerfullest. The day is over, and he is generally in his most expansive mood. Conversation is never difficult – a book, a picture, an event of the day provide an opening – and most boys are ready to talk freely when they are not in the critical presence of their equals. I try too to make the talk as unofficial as possible, and never to scold or talk about work; but on the other hand, if any serious thing has occurred, it is easy then to say a few friendly words about it.

Of course, the time is limited, and it is a temptation to stay longer with boys who are bursting with questions and information. But to contrive to see all the boys alone for a minute or two is possible, and it is, I believe, one of the most valuable pieces of work that one can do. How this can be done in the schools with the dormitory system it is hard to say, but it ought to be schemed for. It is not at all the same thing to send for a succession of boys to the study, however easy may be the talk when they get there, because a boy is apt to feel that there must be trouble brewing. I suppose that having boys in quietly to meals would be a substitute; but the brief morning meal with letters and the paper is not very sociable. Besides, the essence of the situation is that the boy is in his own stronghold, and has not to assume company manners.

I generally stroll into the house in the course of the long evenings for a few minutes; but that is a different kind of thing, because then boys are apt to be congregated together, and the conversation has to be general and of a supposed humorous nature.

In any case the relations should be paternal and not sentimental. It is the temptation of some men, and especially of celibates, to feel a kind of tenderness for what is young and bright and attractive; but boys are quick to notice and resent any favouritism, and one of the first resolves a master must make is to be scrupulously just. No boy resents a master seeing rather more of brisk and lively boys, if they are certain that their brisk companions will not gain any official advantages by private friendship. Affection of an elderly and sensible kind is intensely appreciated, and very few boys will risk a collision with a master if it means a rupture of pleasant relations.

As the boys get older it is important to remember that there should be an increase of respectfulness imported into the manner of a schoolmaster, and that they should be addressed as equals. A course of action, the exercise of discipline should be carefully explained to upper boys, and it is as well if anything serious has occurred to take the elder boys entirely into your confidence and talk about your desires and difficulties as you would discuss them with elder sons. Nothing is so valued by the young as respect; and any approach to confidence on the part of a master in matters where he feels and thinks seriously is deeply valued and respected.

Of course discretion must be used as to what is told to boys; they cannot as a rule keep secrets, even when it is to their own disadvantage that they should be known, but about any matter that it is wise to tell them the utmost frankness of speech is advisable. I do not think it is wise to put too much active responsibility into their hands, but that they should feel some responsibility is entirely good. Of course in intercourse with boys a good deal of tact is necessary; any approach to a liberty must be checked, and can easily be checked by telling a boy that his attitude is no doubt meant for friendliness, but that familiarity is no compliment, and that you do not desire that goodwill should take that form of easiness.

Let me give a very minute instance of an incident where frankness on the part of a master was entirely successful. A friend of mine was accustomed to give the boys a cup of tea and a biscuit before early school. One day another species of biscuit was substituted, and was received with disfavour and rejected; the unhappy biscuits were thrown about, and the boys loudly complained to the servants and each other that they had nothing fit to eat. A rigid man would have made a fuss, punished the offenders, and probably insisted on the unpopular biscuits being eaten. But my friend sent for the majority of the boys, and told them plainly that the particular meal was not in the school dietary, but entirely of his own providing. He said that it was paid for entirely out of his own pocket, and that it was as bad taste to behave as they had done as if they have been invited to a meal by a friend and had done the same thing. He then said that he had ordered the original biscuit to be restored. All this was said good-humouredly, but plainly. The result was that not only was there no diminution of friendliness, but that two upper boys came to him as a deputation and said that it was the general wish that the despised biscuit should be retained.

Another requisite is courtesy in dealing with boys. That is to a great extent a question of manner, but it can be sedulously practised and is never thrown away. Of course it should be natural and not elaborate. But the real secret of satisfactory relations with boys is after all to study the individual, and to adapt yourself accordingly. It is a pity to treat all boys alike and in a professional manner. The more you know of a boy, of his home, of his relations and himself, the easier does a friendly understanding become. It is as well, too, to get the fullest possible account of new boys from their private school masters, and I have always found the latter most ready and willing to give all the assistance in their power. Again, it is of infinite importance that the boy should feel that you are on easy terms with his parents, and it is as important to cultivate relations with the parents as with the boys. No doubt parents and boys discuss the characteristics of their master, and if the parents of a boy speak of the boy's housemaster with friendliness and respect, the boy transfers the master into the family circle, and then the master can adopt the position which is the best in every way – that of a relation, whose affection is of a paternal character and undoubted, and whose authority is unquestioned.

Perhaps a few words may here be said upon the relations

between a parent and a schoolmaster; the only satisfactory basis is that of mutual confidence, tempered by discretion. The dangers which tend to make the relations difficult are twofold. A parent has very often a not unnatural mistrust of a schoolmaster, or, to put it more delicately, he has not full confidence in the schoolmaster's discretion. He feels that if he talks freely, the schoolmaster may use what he says for disciplinary purposes, and that his boy may eventually be placed in a disagreeable position. The fear that a schoolmaster will act inconsiderately and incriminate a boy, who will thereupon be ostracised by other boys, will often keep a parent silent when he ought to speak; and it may frankly be admitted that schoolmasters are not always discreet in this matter. On the other hand, the schoolmaster is often in a somewhat difficult position, because he is in the position of a Tribune, has to try and see that equal justice is done to all the boys under his care, and can hardly let an evil alone of which he knows. Yet, after all, where both a parent and a master sincerely desire the good of the boy, there is not likely to be any very serious difference of opinion.

The only attitude on the part of a parent which is frankly to be deplored is when he takes the line that the boy is sent to school to be taught what is necessary, to be kept respectable or even made creditable; that this is the schoolmaster's business, and that he is not bound to give any assistance himself in the matter. Such a parent perhaps indulges the boy in small things, such as smoking or the unrestricted use of wine, which, if not undesirable for boys in themselves, are at any rate deliberately excluded from the system of public schools. He laughs at the stories of schoolboy pranks, he is anxious that the boy should not be found out, and at the same time that he should pose as a lad of spirit; he enjoys the recital of the grotesque peculiarities of the boy's tutor and his feeble guilelessness.

Such an attitude is perhaps not common, but it is not unknown. Although a master of strong will may maintain a hold over a boy whose parents are indifferent in the matter, if the boy is naturally affectionate and ingenuous, yet no schoolmaster can possibly do more than control a boy whose home background is such as I have described, if the boy is by nature cynical, malevolent or low-minded.

A celebrated statesman was once said to venerate the institution of episcopacy and to dislike a bishop. There are similarly a certain number of parents who admire the public school system and ridicule a schoolmaster. One does not desire a hypocritical attitude, that a parent should keep up an absurd post of veneration for a schoolmaster whom he may suspect to be a fool and know to be a weak man. But though the case I have depicted above is an extreme one, yet if parents did cultivate more cordial relations with schoolmasters, tried to do their good points justice, cordially co-operated with them, provided they were once assured of the master's goodwill and discretion, the result would be a gain in the tone of public school life, because there is nothing more easy than to help and influence a boy, if you are perfectly certain – and I can thankfully add that this has generally been my own experience – that a parent will warmly endorse any policy that you believe to be for the boy's good, and take for granted that a master has the boy's interest at heart.

# X

# ATHLETICS

It is above all things important that education should not be
wholly at the mercy of a prevalent tendency. The schools of a
country are bound to a certain extent to reflect the ideas of desires
of that country, but it is essential that great institutions should
have a philosophical ideal, a tradition of their own, which should
not be stubbornly conservative, but which at the same time
should not be merely indicative of the *popularis aura*, like a
fluctuating vane swinging idly in the wind. What is needed is a
statesmanlike view, swift to welcome and encourage any
wholesome and beneficial impulse, but at the same time to resist
wisely, gently, and secretly the overwhelming force of fashion.

There is no tendency which ought to be more carefully
watched and guarded than our present athletic ideals, which
have taken so firm a hold of the country. A rough test of the
popularity of athletic pursuits is the number of daily papers
which are almost wholly concerned with athletic matters, as
well as the large share which they claim even of great dailies. It
is apt to disconcert the philosophical mind to find a leading
evening paper displacing the war news for a column,
introduced by prodigious headlines, recording the performance
of an English team of cricketers in Australia.

Now it is simply fantastic to set one's face obstinately against
this wave of feeling, to assume that it is utterly and entirely
frivolous, childish, and absurd for a great nation to attach such
importance to such things. It was characteristic of Athens at the
time of her brightest political eminence, when her writers were
pondering with careless ease works which have given a literary
standard to the most keenly intellectual periods ever since, and

are at once the wonder and despair of creative minds, to attach a similar importance to athletic pursuits. It is not therefore a state of things inconsistent with high political and intellectual fervour, though it may not now coexist with those things in England.

On the other hand, there is no doubt a certain danger in the tendency. Boys brought up under the influence of an overwhelming preponderance of athletics are apt to lose the balance and proportion of mind and life altogether. To think that athletic distinction is the one thing worth living for is to lay plans for life as though it ended at thirty.

It is dangerous again for boys to feel that the swiftest and surest way to eminence is through athletics. There is a deep-seated thirst for personal distinction in most active-minded boys; and to gain the badges of athletic merit, in the shape of caps and other trophies, to wear them with solemn pride before others not so fortunate, to see their names in the papers as the makers of long scores, to appear before the public at metropolitan cricket grounds – all this naturally tends to cast a glamour over athletics which is very potent indeed. The danger would be inconsiderable if we could depend upon matters righting themselves as soon as the boys entered upon the sober business of the world; but now that athletic pursuits can be and are prolonged into middle life, the contact with the workaday world does not necessarily undeceive a man.

Of course, the athletic system has great and obvious advantages: it gives health and healthful occupation to boys at a time when they are both desiderata; it confers on boys certain manly qualities – presence of mind, the self-possession which enables a person to play an unconcerned part in the presence of his fellows; it may produce, though it does not always produce, serenity under defeat, the sacrifice of self to the interests of a side, power of leadership, obedience, hardiness, and many

51

other valuable things. But the danger at present is that the system does not tend to produce the due subordination of self, but only the intense desire to be personally distinguished in these matters. I once asked a good many boys to tell me candidly whether they would prefer to gain great distinction in a match and have their side beaten, or that their side should win, but that they themselves should be discredited; and I can only say that very few indeed chose the latter alternative.

Moreover, it used to be asserted that athletics were valuable from a moral point of view, and kept physical temptations at bay. I do not think that this can be maintained, and I am sure that the personal popularity which the athlete enjoys, the almost adoration with which he is often regarded, is of itself a great danger if a boy is prone to sensual faults.

I do not here propose to discuss the respective merits of different kinds of games; I only desire to trace what the attitude of schoolmasters should be towards games.

It is of course undeniable that a successful athletic career is of itself a high qualification for the position of a schoolmaster. Games are so carefully organised, so integral a part of school life, that it is necessary to have competent persons who can give them supervision, and whose record is one which the boys will respect. It is, moreover, a healthy thing and promotes general good feeling that the masters should take part in the games of the school, though I confess that it seems to me somewhat undignified for the masters, as is the case in many private schools, to be as vigorously on duty out of school as in, and to be practically little more than professionals in hours of recreation.

A man who comes to school as a competent athlete finds his path smoothed for him from the first, and the boys are ready to give him the prompt obedience which admiration encourages, especially if they feel that they can consult him out of school on the object that is of the greatest importance to themselves. But I am on the other hand quite sure that the athletic qualification is not the only title to respect. I may perhaps quote a personal experience; I was for a few years a competent football player, when I first went to a public school as a master, until a bad accident put an end, once and for all, to my appearance in that capacity. I admit that I had attached considerable importance to the fact that I could take a part from time to time in school matches, and I feared that I might find that it would become harder without it to maintain my position, such as it was, with the boys. But I have not found that my retirement has made any perceptible difference – indeed, two seasons after my retirement I found the boys were entirely unaware that I had ever been a football player at all.

The mistake that is often made by schoolmasters is to put themselves too much on a level with the boys in these matters. Of course if a man is frankly absorbed in athletics himself, and makes no secret of the fact that two rounds of golf a day are as important and integral a part of his life as meals and sleep, it is hard for him to attempt to regulate the feelings of the boys on the subject. But I am strongly of opinion that the interest of masters in games should be of the paternal kind; that the boys should feel that the interest the masters take in the games is not the interest of the partisan or the expert, so much as the personal interest which they take in all that concerns the boys for whom they are responsible.

I cannot indicate how this should be made clear to the boys unless it is actually there; but I am quite clear that if the interest which a master took in games was of this sort, the fact would be soon appreciated by the boys; and I think it is very important that the boys should feel, not in an oppressive or priggish way, but as a thing that is absolutely natural and right, that their masters have somewhat more extended interests, and are occupied with somewhat larger considerations than the exact merits of each member of the team or the boat.

Of course I do not recommend a Jesuitical subtlety in the matter. I do not desire that the hopes and fears and ideals of the masters should be mainly and candidly athletic, and that they should scheme to conceal this from the boys, and should be always drawing morals and pointing to higher things – though I do not think that this old-fashioned function of the parent and the schoolmaster is somewhat unduly depressed – but what I contend for is that the masters should have wider interests and bigger ideas, and that while they do not conceal from the boys that this is the case, the boys should at the same time see that such things are not in the least inconsistent with a very real and active interest in sports and pastimes.

The danger throughout is that what is meant for amusement and health is getting to be taken altogether too seriously. Success in games is so ardently desired, it is so much identified with success in school life, that one knows of boys who suffer in health and have sleepless nights when their cricket goes off – boys who are entirely and deeply thankful for a rainy day in the cricket season because it gives them a day free from the burden of a horrible anxiety. When it is reduced to this, it is patent to all that things are not in an entirely satisfactory position; and though it may be said that the position of athletics is now too firmly established to be worth tilting against, and that the man who resists the dominant athletic tendency is a mere Don Quixote, I cannot believe that it is so, or that schoolmasters are right in falling so completely in with the current.

It brings me back to a former conclusion, that a schoolmaster ought not to be content to think that he has done his duty, if he has spent a day in which he has taught firmly his prescribed subject, insisting on the tale of work; has looked on at or taken part in some match or contest in the afternoon, and has discussed with heat and enthusiasm the athletic topics of the day, the precise shades of superiority which the play of a particular boy or a particular master has shown, and perhaps arrived at maturer views of the same question over a midnight pipe. It is difficult to say exactly at what point he has failed in his duty; but I would contend that the game over, the requisite freshness of body attained, there ought to be other subjects which he is ready and anxious to attack, there ought to be books he desires to read, or points that he is disposed to discuss; and I would maintain that the master who, having spent such a day as I have described, lays his head on the pillow in a perfectly virtuous and self-satisfied frame of mind is possibly to be envied, as we might envy a dog who curls himself up in his basket with a happy sigh after a vigorous day, but he is not less certainly both *borné* and mistaken in his view of the balance and proportion of life.

# XI

# TIME

One of the perennial difficulties in the assiduous schoolmaster's way is the question of time – how to gain it, how to use it. It generally happens in other professions that a man as he rises in it has more leisure; the simply drudgery is spared him, he can choose more what he likes, he can do the part of his work that he prefers, he can leave details to his subordinates. But the precise opposite is the case with schoolmasters. When a man first goes to a school as a master, his duty is simply to teach a division; as his work goes on, other things are gradually put into his hand; he becomes a tutor, he gives special instruction, he takes up special subjects, he undertakes the supervision of some school department, he manages some athletic business, he discharges secretarial duties, he controls a workshop or a gymnasium, he audits accounts – one of the many public services that have to be done by someone, and which, though not compulsory, are apt to be pressed upon active men. Then comes a boarding-house, and a whole class of new duties falls into the hands of a schoolmaster, and these as a rule continue to the end.

How to deal with this; how to secure some time for reading, for recollection, for thought – this is a problem which weighs upon some men very heavily, though it must be confessed that it does not weigh upon all alike, because it is very common to find active men without originative power, men who like to have tasks set them, and are happiest when every moment is filled with small and definite duties.

Of course it is a great thing that there should be men of this practical, willing type at a school, but it is not the only type, and, while schoolmasters are educators, it is impossible to insist too strongly upon their duty to be intellectually alive.

The problem is easy of solution in the case of men who do their work rapidly; men of great intellectual concentration and decisive views can get through exercises and papers with great rapidity, and do them very fair justice too. But these are rare; and I am sure that the schoolmaster is often in danger of being immersed in detailed work from the beginning to the end of the school term, work which he may perform conscientiously, but without animation; and then, although he may be respected and though he may exact solid work from the boys, he is not likely to communicate any enthusiasm. A boy does not feel enthusiastic when he takes an exercise carefully underlined from the hands of a tired master, but when he feels himself in contact with a vigorous mind.

A great deal can be done by pure and simple method; if a man makes definite rules for himself, and keeps them mechanically, an immense saving can always be effected. He should settle with himself his hours of sleep, his hours of recreation; and if time is thus methodised and arranged, and if dawdling, irresolute habits are strenuously avoided, it is surprising to find how much time remains. If one adds up carefully all the hours of the day that are spent in definite occupations, and subtracts the amount from twenty-four hours, it is almost shocking to discover how large a margin there is.

The key of the situation is to be found in the simple fact that a man has always time for anything that he desires sufficiently to do; work gets itself done in the most astonishing way if one has only a suppressed desire in the background to be at it; and it is clear that as a rule the principal reason which keeps a man from reading, writing, private work of any kind in a busy life is not that he is too busy, but that he does not really want to do it.

A great bishop lately dead, who was for fifteen years a public school master, told me that he had never been able to do so much theological work when a bishop as he had been able to do when he was a schoolmaster, though he had as much or more leisure time, for the simple reason that he had known exactly, as a schoolmaster, what his free spaces were, and that if he did not use them fully he must wait until the next interval.

A man is justified in resolutely guarding against interruptions in the hours which he consecrates to private work; he ought to be accessible at certain hours of the day, but there will be times when the only interruptions to be feared are casual callers, and against such invasions he may erect a fence of habit and deliberate seclusion.

For instance, on a half-holiday afternoon there is often a pleasant interval between exercise and work. If exercise is soberly taken, so as to refresh without fatiguing, a man's mental powers are at their very best at such a time. It is tempting to the natural man to sip tea, to talk, to reflect, to turn over the pages of a book, to slumber; but I have found by experience that it is possible to cultivate a feeling of intense jealousy about these hours and to retire into solitude, which is absolutely forbidden to invade except in a case of extreme necessity, and that the hours thus guarded add up very rapidly. The books read accumulate; the little manuscript grows – and this without trenching on hours of definite work, without rendering a man unsociable, without destroying possibilities of exercise.

One difficulty arises from letters. As life goes on one's correspondence tends to grow; I can only say that rapidity in dealing with letters should be religiously cultivated, and moreover the habit of using up fragments of time. A great many of a schoolmaster's letters are merely small questions of detail. An important or an anxious letter must of course be dealt with at leisure. There are many little contrivances too which help a man to do work of this kind expeditiously – materials at hand everywhere, care and method in the arrangement of papers, and so forth.

If I hear a man complain that there is no time for anything but work, I feel sure that one of the above characteristics is wanting – that he is either unmethodical, or that the central desire is wanting. I am quite sure from experience that the latter is generally the case. If the desire is strong enough, the work is done; and, again, the presence of an active desire, the having on hand work of a kind which is a pleasure and to which a man turns with avidity, is in itself the most potent influence to make a man methodical.

# XII

# HOLIDAYS

Much might be said about the wise use of holidays. They are, of course, a time of storage – storage of health and vigour and interest, and all the things on which there is a heavy drain in the school-time.

In the first place there should be plenty of open air and exercise, especially for men of a sedentary habit, who should take exercise patiently and philosophically as a tonic. But the schoolmaster's life is not a sedentary one, and the holiday should not be consecrated to exercise pure and simple, because one of the obvious advantages of the schoolmaster's life is that exercise, and even violent exercise, can easily be obtained.

I do not think that there is any excuse for schoolmasters making the holidays a kind of physical debauch; and the man who spends the daylight hours of his holiday on cricket, or golf, or mountain climbing, and the rest of his time in gossip, or cards, or billiards, may come back to his work in what he considers good physical condition, but he will not return to routine with any willingness, but rather in a state of irritation at the restraints it is going to impose upon him.

What a schoolmaster should rather aim at in the holidays is change and variety. He should certainly rest in the first place. Charles Kingsley used to say that when he broke down in health from overwork he used to rush off and indulge in violent forms of physical exercise, and was often surprised to find how slowly he recovered. Later in life he learnt that what he had been doing was merely substituting one kind of strain for another, and that a wise passiveness was the best beginning, gradually increasing physical exercise as the holiday advanced.

In the matter, for instance, of sleep, a schoolmaster is often rather apt, rising early and going to bed late as he does, to have large arrears to make up, and sleep is a matter of idiosyncrasy. Mr Gladstone used to say that the old rule of seven hours for a man, eight hours for a woman, and nine for a fool, was the silliest piece of absurdity ever framed; and to a schoolmaster who has worked hard, long hours of bed in the holidays are often highly valuable.

Some people like travel, some like visiting, some like a leisurely home life in familiar scenes; and, for rest, it is of great importance that a man should enjoy the prospect of whatever he is going to do. But two things are certain: that for a man whose time for reading is limited, and whose work is intellectual, there should be a serious attempt to read something to stir and fill the mind.

Then, too, the schoolmaster should avoid, as a general rule, the society of his colleagues in the holidays. He should wash his mind clear of worries and anxieties and familiar questions. He should try and set himself in line with the outer world, and put his cramped mind in easier positions. He should try and see something of general society, and of men and women whose view of life is not the same as his own. He should be apt to visit at the homes of some of his pupils, if he is asked to do so. There is no hold so valuable on boys as the hold which comes of intimacy with their parents, and some idea as to how their lives are conditioned. It is good to revisit the University, it is good to visit London; the best thing is to have some general scheme of interest and theory, and to fit the details according to taste.

Of course, the above applies mainly to the unmarried schoolmaster. A married schoolmaster has enough to do to try and pick up the threads of his own broken domestic life. But the general result should be that a man should return to his work in good spirits, fresh, and with his head full of new schemes and experiments, anxious to see his boy-friends, and with a pleasant store of holiday experiences.

I do not believe that it is a fair thing to one's profession to work too hard in the holidays. The temptation is great to an ardent sightseer to travel feverishly about and to try and press a great deal into the time; the man who is interested in literary work is apt to immerse himself in writing; the philanthropist or the evangelist is inclined to study problems, or to make his voice heard in the pulpit. But though the main thing is that the holidays should be spent in a congenial way, it is a bad thing to feel that the coming term is an interruption of one's real preferences. If a man feels this, and feels it constantly, he had better begin to reflect whether he is in his place as a schoolmaster at all, and whether he had not better adopt a line of activity more consonant with his tastes and desires; because schoolmastering is not only a trade or a profession, it is an art; and if a man feels that his heart is not in his work, but elsewhere, he had better, even at the sacrifice of worldly prospects, resolutely make up his mind to employ himself more where his treasure is. This may seem unpractical advice; but there is no sadder or more deadening thing than to go back to a profession which bores you, without interest or zeal, unless, indeed, a man is in the unhappy position of having neither enthusiasm nor preferences; and in this case it is not even conscientious to pursue, unwillingly and heavily, a profession on which the minds and characters and futures of so many human beings depend.

# XIII

# SOCIABILITY

The sociability of masters among themselves is a very important question. I suppose it is inevitable that at the majority of schools the common-room system should prevail, on the ground of economy; but it brings with it obvious and undeniable evils which are absent from societies where the common life is not so insistent. It is hardly to be hoped that men, possibly irritable and probably tired, should meet day after day at meals without engendering a certain amount of friction; and possibly the institution of silent meals, as in monastic life, might be useful, if feasible. In a close society all sorts of little things get on sensitive nerves. The tones of certain voices, the familiar turns of remarks, ancient stories, methods of dealing with food, small personal characteristics, are apt to grate on perceptions stimulated by irritability. I am sure that it is a good thing that masters should be, if possible, in separate lodgings, and that they should not meet more than once in the day, if it can be so arranged without undue expense. But if they must meet, nothing but the exercise of resolute good-humour, deliberate courtesy, careful tact, can possibly minimise the evil. If masters can breakfast alone, and can take a midday meal with the boys, they ought to be able to meet once a day without undue friction; and the occasional presence of the headmaster at these gatherings doubtless would tend to preserve harmony. At the same time it is probable that there will be some masterful, prejudiced man of quick speech who will inevitably give a good deal of pain to his colleagues. A stubborn insistence on opinions, the expression of contempt for other people's views, are difficult to avoid in such societies. I have heard of pathetic and melancholy scenes that have taken place at these gatherings. I have heard of an assistant-master of æsthetic tastes saying in a fretful voice, during a pause in the rich tide of shop, "We sit here day after day, and the name of Ruskin is not even mentioned!" I have heard of masters condemned to meet week after week at the common meal who were not on speaking terms with each other, and never communicated except in acid notes. I have heard of a young man, new to his work, listening to a room which was separated into two eager groups, one of which was discussing the relative size of their class-rooms, and the other the portion of the human frame best adapted for the infliction of corporal punishment.

Of course the trivialities of ordinary intercourse are very distressing; there must be trivialities indeed, and it is impossible for men living a common life with common interests not to indulge largely in 'shop'. But I think that masters ought deliberately to attempt to keep the tone of such gatherings good-humoured, if not intelligent. And if each member of the party were convinced of the necessity of doing so, the conquest would be an easy one.

Apart from that, each master should try to see something of his fellows in private, to understand them, to admire their good points, to sympathise with them. At the school which I serve the social question is comparatively easy. The masters live separate, except for small 'rookeries' of two or three junior masters, which associations are generally determined by private friendship. Small, brief dinner-parties are often given by housemasters, where one meets one's fellows on the pleasantest terms, and a man who is willing to spend a little money on entertaining does not throw it away. It makes, moreover, a great difference, trivial though it may appear, that evening dress is habitually worn. The man dressed for dinner puts on with his armour a certain deliberate courtesy; and though it might be rather troublesome, I believe that it would be a gain if this were adopted at common-room gatherings. Indeed, I think it is an important thing, both from the point of view of boys and colleagues, that slovenliness of dress and demeanour should be sedulously avoided. But a master's life is too busy for any great sociability, and general society is one of the things that he must cheerfully make up his mind to forego. But it is astonishing how the dinner parties I have alluded to make for peace and mutual understanding. It is difficult to quarrel with a man who has sat next to you at dinner and made himself agreeable. And what is more important still, it is well that boys should feel that the masters are friends and allies among themselves, not in the spirit of a Trades Union, but for the best of human reasons. It is impossible, and I think undesirable, that masters should never speak to boys, or boys to masters, of other masters; indeed I think that a master who is not afraid to speak of the good points of his colleagues to boys smooths the way for them very considerably. Of course mere gossip should be avoided; but it is only natural for human beings who meet constantly to talk to each other of the people in whom they are interested; and to lay down a hard and fast rule about silence on such points, is to keep up that sour and grim mystery, the mystery of the 'buckram', which has prevailed too long in English school life. Of course tact is needed, and a master should lay down for himself a general principle that it is undesirable for him to gossip to boys about other masters; but I am quite sure that it is a principle and not a rule, and that great benefits may result from a master being willing to explain another master to a boy in a kindly, human way. Boys will be sure to discuss masters among themselves, and it is better that they should have some true facts to go upon,

rather than the very superficial impression that they will
themselves form.

# XIV

# RELIGION

It is undoubtedly true that Englishmen are apt to be reticent about religious matters. A great many people share the opinion of the sage who, on being asked what his religion was, replied that he was of the religion of all sensible men; and on being pressed to define it more particularly, he went on to say that it was what all sensible men kept to themselves.

If the average Englishman is not very keenly interested in the superficial or rather technical aspect of religion; if he is somewhat contemptuous of the so-called science of worship, liturgical tradition; if he does not take a very active interest in dogmatic religion or in metaphysical processes, he is, I believe, very deeply interested in the essentials of religion. I think that there is a very deep attachment in the minds of English people to the principles of Justice, Mercy, and Truth; a strong national instinct for duty and manly living. Perhaps the poetical side of religion, the beauty of holiness, the sense of mystical communion, the reveries of faith, the spirit of symbolism, the attitude of reverence are not as dear as they might be to the Anglo-Saxon character.

But it is better to cultivate existing virtues than to endeavour to create those that do not rest upon a natural instinct; and a master has faith enough to appeal to in the solid sense of duty which is undoubtedly present in the mind of the majority of English boys.

English boys moreover, like English men, have a strong sense of appropriateness in the matter of religion; and though a man of strong and simple religious feeling might talk often and frankly to boys on religious subjects without being misunderstood, yet any attempt to do this as a matter of duty and not as a matter of instinct would be apt to render a man liable to be considered sanctimonious – a quality which at once alienates respect.

In one way, too, a boy's sense of reverence is very strong; he dislikes the feelings which lie deep being dragged habitually to the surface. I remember, for instance, the case of a pupil of my own who was prepared for confirmation by an excellent clergyman connected with the school. After the confirmation was over the clergyman asked the boy to tea with him, and complained to me some time after that the boy never came. This seemed to me so odd that I questioned the boy about it, and it turned out that he was afraid the clergyman would want to pray with him. He had heard that he had done so with a boy who went to tea, and someone had come in in the middle and found them on their knees; and the prospect was one which he could not face.

On the other hand, at the right time and place boys are only too ready to listen to religious talk and to be grateful for it. I have never found boys anything but interested in a religious application to practical life made in the course of a divinity lesson. But all attempt to touch on religious subjects in private life should be made with infinite tact and judgement.

The preparation for confirmation is the one great opportunity that a schoolmaster has for talking of religious matters to his boys; and I believe it to be not only a right principle that a boy's housemaster or tutor should have the opportunity of preparing a boy, but that it is a duty which no housemaster or tutor should avoid except for the gravest reasons. Of course if a man feels that his faith is so far divergent from the orthodox faith of the Gospel as to make it impossible for him to speak with any conviction on sacred subjects, he can hardly conscientiously accept the task of instructing a boy; but if he holds the cardinal doctrines of the Christian faith, he ought not to allow any *mauvaise honte* or any consideration of personal unworthiness to stand in his way.

In the first place it is the best natural opportunity that a master has for making it clear to the boy that he does feel religion to be a vital matter, and that it lies at the back of his life-work; and as to personal unworthiness, it is surely possible for a man to say frankly to a boy that he speaks not as one who triumphed over difficulties and has experienced the fullest powers of the faith of Christ, but as one who is an elder disciple, a little ahead in point of time, at all events, upon the road which leads to God, who at any rate sees clearly what he believes to be true, though his practice may fall far short of it. It appears to me that such an appeal, if sincerely made, may be far more potent than an appeal made, so to speak, from some higher platform.

I believe that in preparing boys for confirmation it is better to keep instruction and practical counsels apart in one sense. That is to say that I believe that the boys should be clearly and simply instructed together in doctrinal teaching, and that the basis of all such instruction should be the Apostles' Creed. And that they should then be addressed together or separately on practical points of life and religion, but that the teacher should be very careful never to leave a doctrinal statement to stand alone without afterwards showing how it can and ought to affect life and action. Thus the thought of God as the Almighty Creator should be expanded into the feeling of an utter dependence both in physical and material things on causes that lie outside our own control.

Care, too, should I think be taken to make such preparation dignified as well as simple. A worthy schoolmaster was once asked how he prepared the boys for confirmation. "Oh," he said, "I just tell them to buck up." Even if he did not employ this precise formula in his private talks, one cannot help feeling that such preparation should be conducted in a more reverent and delicate manner. A good many boys have an instinctive sense of the beauty of holiness, and an appeal may well be made to higher tones of feeling, and motives may be indicated of a deeper kind than those which can be dealt with in the schoolroom or the street.

I believe that each man must settle for himself whether it is better to see boys together or separately. Of course some topics should be treated of separately; but here again a man should discover how is most effective; and in a busy life, with a large number of boys to prepare, it is impossible I think with any freshness to say practically the same things over and over again, perhaps half a dozen times in the course of the evening. But if boys are prepared together, great care should be taken to give each as far as possible a feeling of seclusion; to assemble boys, as used to be done, in a schoolroom, and to read lectures out of a note-book is almost ideally ineffective. Boys are greatly ruled by outside impressions, and it is of great importance that a man should change the *venue* where such instruction is concerned; and that he should speak easily and without notes – even if he loses some exactness by so doing – and in a room where each boy can feel that he is not under the inspection of the other boys in the class.

These, however, are matters of detail and idiosyncrasy. The principle is that masters should not any account neglect the opportunity. Supposing that a master is a layman and that the parents desire a clerical preparation, the master should make a point of seeing the boy and making him feel that his own interest in the question is a vital one.

Moreover, a few words on religious matters may well be spoken seriously to boys when they are leaving school, when the heart is warm, and when the most eager temperaments are dimly over-shadowed by the thought of the larger world, on the threshold of which they stand.

Personal religion among boys is far higher and more common than it used to be a few years ago. I find that comparatively few boys altogether neglect prayer and Bible reading; but at my own school there is the advantage of boys being in separate rooms.

There remains the question of the chapel service; and here we are on more difficult ground. The great majority of boys come from homes where the idea of attending a daily service would appear merely fantastic; and then the daily chapel service is very easily looked upon as a mere school formality. From the master's point of view, the school chapel service should be at a time when masters can attend easily and as a matter of course; and it is thus better if possible to make it follow or immediately precede a school, so that there is no waste of time in going and returning. It should also be short and varied; there should be a little simple singing; but such a service as the Litany should, I think, be avoided. It is quite true that it may be a valuable discipline for boys to try and exercise themselves in following, in mind and voice, a service of a monotonous kind; but how many boys avail themselves of this discipline? And how can the success of the experiment be tested? Some men seem to believe that a practice is good and valuable so long as it is tedious, on the principle that 'they also serve who only stand and wait'. I can only say that of my own contemporaries at school, where twice a week the service consisted of the Litany, few ever claimed to have got any good out of the service so arranged, or to have derived any faculty from it except the unhappy one of isolating the attention from what is proceeding in your presence.

The liturgical faculty is a rare one, and requires careful training. To be able to give an uplifted attention to a series of short petitions is a very difficult matter. If you are tempted to meditate for a moment on any one petition, you are lost; the service flows on, and you have to take it up again where you find it; on the other hand, a mechanical and Pharisaical attention is not a difficult accomplishment. But who would say that it had any very great spiritual effect?

I would plead therefore for as much variety as is consistent with liturgical usage in services for boys. A psalm and a hymn would naturally be sung and a lesson read, but I think it is a great pity that out of the great storehouse that exists of prayers, both ancient and modern, some should not be used in such services as I describe, where the congregation is young and so dependent upon variety, so untrained to bear the stress of liturgical asceticism. Not to travel far for instances, there are many prayers of exquisite beauty in the works of Jeremy Taylor; and it would not be difficult to draw up a little volume of additional collects for use in school chapels which would infinitely enrich the services. It must be borne in mind that the daily school service is not so much a liturgical ceremony as a family gathering for prayer. Moreover, it should be made a point to secure if possible the services of a really beautiful reader. Impressiveness in reading is not much cultivated in England; but I have heard a clergyman read the exhortation at the beginning of the service in such a way that it seemed to me that I had never known it before; and I have knelt at the side of Mr Gladstone in a Communion Service, and shall never forget the impressiveness of his responses to the commandments, the simple fervour with which he made each petition his own.

Again, as to preaching at schools, it is as well, I believe, that the bulk of the preaching should be done by the men concerned in the work of the place, and that great care should be taken about the sermons by those in authority. The quality of shrewdness, the wisdom of serpents of which our Lord spoke, is the quality most often lacking in all our pulpits, but the men who are best acquainted with the life of the place are the most likely to be able to lay their fingers on the weak points. School sermons should be rigorously short; and external preachers should not be invited unless they are of proved eminence. An intelligent boy once complained to me that the sermons of strange preachers were as a rule devoted either to the question of purity, or to imploring the boys to become clergymen, or both; and I thus think it would be as well if the subjects were carefully laid down beforehand, so that some conspectus of Christian life might be attempted. If there are two sermons on a Sunday, which is undesirable, I believe that courses of exposition would be found advantageous in the morning at all events; or the religious instruction given by masters might be devoted to going through the services for the day, and endeavouring to make it clear to the boys what they will hear and say and sing: *Psallam et mente.*

I read the other day of a worthy parish clergyman whose services were the delight of his parish. He was very paternal in manner; he would say after reading a few verses of a psalm that the psalm was a very difficult one, and that he would ask the congregation to sit down while he explained it; "and I shall put aside," he would add, "the sermon that I have written for you to-day, and make my sermon out of this, and when we have understood the psalm, we will say it all together heartily and intelligently." He would go so far, said his biographer, as to suit his action to the word on occasions; and when reading such a psalm as 'O clap your hands together, all ye people', he would clap his hands together with vigorous illustration.

Of course, the above method requires a mixture of originality and dignity which is rare; but I cannot help believing that a certain similar informality might well be introduced into school services.

I do not at all believe in making the service too 'boyish' in character. I well remember the dislike I felt as a child to being made to sing children's hymns. I did not like to sing *We are but little children weak*, because I did not feel weak, and I did not wish to be reminded that I was; still more offensive was being made to sing about my 'little hands'. I did not think them little, and I did not see why they should be made the subject of general remark. Such hymns are more for the pleasure of elder people, who are charmed by the sight of innocence and weakness asserting their own claims. But the boy delights to feel himself a pilgrim, a soldier, a hero; and he should be encouraged to feel that his part in the battle is as important as that of his elders.

Some masters like to preach little sermons to the boys of their own house, say on Sunday evenings. I do not believe that the boys need so much exhortation on Sundays, and I think that the pleasure of the orator is sometimes as much a motive as the good of the boys. Moreover, it is much easier to say what you want to individuals than to numbers. Many boys are serious enough when by themselves, but in the presence of other boys they are affected by a kind of false shame, which shuts the doors of the mind upon realities, and concerns itself only with superficial matters.

What is most important of all is to make the boys feel that public worship is a means to an end; that religion is not a separate department of life, a thing for the chapel and the prayer-room, but a force animating the whole of life. If they can be convinced that in the school services they can find an inspiration which enables them to deal with the ordinary temptations and difficulties of life in a sober and enthusiastic spirit, they will value them; but if they only regard them as stately solemnities which they are bound to attend, they will be tempted to believe that they have fulfilled their religious duties by attendance, and that no more thought need to be given to the question. Neither, I think, should too high an ideal be insisted upon; the ideal should be high, but to put very great and sacred motives before the boys for doing very ordinary things for which there are other and simpler motives is like taking the Ark into battle.

One thing is, I believe, very important: nothing should be allowed in any way to compete with the sanctity and solemnity of the Holy Communion. Masters who care for religious things should use diligence to make and keep those boys who have been confirmed communicants. The worst evils of boy life, the sensuality, the greediness, the materialistic views of things, are apt to shrink and die in the presence of that holy and awful mystery; and it may bring a sanctification into life which no amount of instruction or exhortation can effect.

A master, then, should see that his own religion is simple and vital; and though he should not get into the way of babbling easily on religious subjects, he should rid himself of the *mauvaise honte* which prevents so many Englishmen of devout hearts from ever venturing to speak a word to their boys on such subjects.

# XV

# MORALITIES

I would first say a few words about a master's attitude in dealing with lesser offences against strict morality – dishonesty, untruthfulness and so forth. It is very important to avoid exaggeration, and there is a subtle temptation to a master to speak more impressively than he feels in the cause of right. This is particularly unwise in the case of offences such as copying, or the use of cribs, when it is useless to pretend that a boy is condemned by his companions. I do not mean that a master should condescend to accept the verdict of the boy's code in the matter, and treat such offences as merely disciplinary ones. But neither should he strain the contrast too far; let him remember what he would himself have thought of such offences as a boy, and let him try to indicate a motive which, if it is higher than the average view taken by the boy, should at least not be out of his horizon. It is easy to explain that the word of an Englishman is accepted as more likely to be dependable than the oaths of some nations; and that a boy who is in little things constantly and consciously dishonest and untruthful is not likely to be able to throw off such meannesses when he enters the world. Let a master explain to boys that incessant recourse to assistance in work tends to cripple the mind and make it unfit for vigorous application. These are arguments which a boy can understand and appreciate. It is easy to say to a boy who has been guilty of untruthfulness or dishonesty, "I must feel that I can trust what you say, and believe in the honesty of your work; I intend to act upon this supposition, and you must do your part as well." The boy will not feel this to be an exaggerated but a sensible view; he will not be tempted to think it a merely professional statement. There may be boys with whom it is possible to take a higher line; but the thing to be desired is that the arrow should hit the target and not fly over it. It is just as well too to add that in any case it is obvious that such things cannot be permitted from the disciplinary point of view; and that if the boy does not wish to comply for the better reason, it will be necessary to fall back upon the other. I can only say that I have met very few boys who did not, at all events, try to appreciate the better motive.

A few words must now be said upon what is after all the dark shadow on the life of a schoolmaster, his most anxious and saddest preoccupation – I mean the dread of the possibility of the prevalence, or at all events the existence, of moral evil among his boys.

Some masters cut the knot by ignoring the thought as far as possible, and acting with extreme severity if any transgression is brought before them. This I believe to be both unwise and unjust. The age at which boys are at public schools, covering as it does the change from boyhood to manhood, must necessarily be attended with temptations of a peculiar kind. Instincts and impulses, natural and wholesome in themselves, begin to stir in the awakening frame, and at a time when the lesson of moral self-control cannot have been fully learnt. Some few boys are gifted with a happy purity of nature which carries them stainless through the time of trial. Others whose instincts are on the right side will remain pure if the tone of the society around them is pure; some few are not so much deliberately wicked as un-moral. They have perhaps inherited a bias to sensuality, and have not inherited any particular self-reverence or self-control. Such boys will be light-heartedly wicked, and their only conscience will be the fear of penalty. But the schoolmaster must realise that the majority of boys would not deliberately plunge into evil, and would be glad to be saved from themselves in the matter; and his duty is to give them all the help that he can.

The darkest feature of the problem is that the boys' code of honour is such that the master is probably the last person to hear of such evil; and let me say at the outset that it is not for a moment to be thought of that he should encourage the boys to give him information – such a practice is utterly fatal to his influence and to his relations with the boys.

There is also a morbid way of treating the subject. There are certain masters who seem to have the question on the brain, and who suppose, or act as if they supposed, that every boy has to pass through the ordeal of temptations to impurity. My own belief is that the large majority never come within the reach of direct external temptation at all. Boys coming to a public school from certain private schools are warned and cautioned in a way that I believe rather tends to increase the evil by familiarity with the belief in its prevalence, than to diminish it. They hear a voice in every wind, and I have little doubt that to go too minutely into details is an entire mistake from every point of view.

A master should encourage parents to speak to him, if necessary, on the subject in a general way. He should not endeavour to obtain specific information from them, but he should ask them, when opportunity occurs, to tell him frankly if they have any reason to suppose that the tone of the house is unsatisfactory. But any statements that they make should be used with the utmost discretion, because boys are apt, particularly good boys, to exaggerate grossly in the matter, and to believe that other boys are bad without any evidence but that of the merest gossip. Parents will often say that boys can be trusted in the matter, because they have no motive to make things out worse than they are. I can only look back to my own experience of school life and reflect that I supposed many boys to be addicted to evil (whom I now know to have been entirely free from it) for no better reason than that someone had told me so.

I believe myself that when a boy comes to school his housemaster should endeavour to ascertain whether he has come under any evil influences. It is easy enough to begin by asking about conversation, and it is easy enough to see whether the boy knows what is meant. If one has reason to suspect that there is more in the background, a master should endeavour to find out generally whether there has been any contact with evil, reassuring the boy on the question of penal consequences.

The master should then, I think, try to arrive at an understanding with the boy on the matter; should make it plain that he thinks and feels more strongly on the point than on any other point whatever, and that he could not retain in his house any boy whose tone was unsound in this matter. He should say that he intends to ask the boy from time to time whether all goes right, and at the same time make it clear that it is to be on a basis of mutual confidence, and that no information about other boys will be asked for or taken.

Of course, there is no guarantee that a boy will fulfil his part of the compact; but I have little doubt that the thought of it does help many boys to exercise care in the matter, and to take the side which, after all, the majority of boys do desire to take – the side of purity.

The boy should be warned very solemnly of the disastrous consequences of such sin – not in an exaggerated way, and not sacrificing truth to impressiveness – and still more solemnly of the infinite blessings and happiness of keeping modest and pure.

I believe that conversation among the boys on such subjects is a fruitful source of such evil; and I therefore do my best to keep the boys straight on this point. Many boys will tell you frankly whether they have come in the way of evil talk, if they feel quite certain that it will not involve any boy in penal consequences. And I am sure that the only possible plan is to be entirely rigid on this point. Not only should no name be ever asked for or listened to, but great care should be taken to show that the master does not even aim at identifying boys by collateral evidence. Sometimes identification is inevitable; but I can only say that I have never used a statement of this kind or betrayed a confidence, though, of course, if definite evidence is laid before me from some other quarters, an investigation has to be conducted on ordinary lines.

Boys are very forgetful creatures, and the impression in the earlier years of school life should not be allowed to fade. I do not fail to ask younger boys, especially those who are likely to be exposed to temptation, who make friendships easily and widely, two or three times in a half whether they are on the right path, and to repeat as seriously as I can how earnestly I desire a pure tone in the house – desire it indeed far beyond any other thing.

It is possible that this plan is not wholly successful; it is impossible to test it accurately; but I have reason to believe that it helps to keep a right tone alive, and minimises the evil.

If once a good tone can be secured, it is possible to make it a matter of pride that it should be maintained. If one can truthfully say to boys that the house has a good reputation in the matter, many boys will, without any affectation of superior goodness, be interested in trying to keep it so. But on the other hand no schoolmaster can ever feel secure on the point, and security is likely to be a fool's paradise, as one really unscrupulous, clever, evil boy may spread corruption wholesale without a master suspecting it.

As a boy gets older and more independent, it will be less necessary to ask questions; but I think that a master may well speak occasionally to his upper boys on the subject, and let them feel how much he has the matter at heart.

I do not believe at all in speaking to boys collectively, either in sermons or addresses on the point; still less in entering into details. Such conversation should be individual and private, and carefully adapted to the temperament of the boy to whom it is addressed.

To speak to boys collectively on such subjects is like trying to fill a number of pitchers by splashing water over them from a pail; each should be separately dipped.

The point to be firmly kept in view is this: that a master has little right to maintain in this matter the attitude of a virginal modesty, affronted, scandalised, and injured by the least violation of the ideal, and avenging it, if such violation occur, with furious contempt and loathing for the accursed thing; but he should rather sorrowfully feel that temptation is strong and that boys are weak, yet that they are in their better moments earnestly and pathetically desirous to be kept from evil, and that no help that he can give is ever thrown away.

I think – I wish I could say otherwise – that any attempt to condone the evil, to give a boy a chance to recover his character in a case where he has gone wrong, is a mistake. Boys are very inquisitive; and a boy who has fallen, and whose fall is known to others, is very likely to revert to evil when the impression of discovery is obliterated. But every care should be taken, every possible precaution, to avoid such a fall prejudicing a boy's future. Indeed, it does not deserve so terrible a punishment. And it is hard to resist a sense of injustice at a sin which often represents far more of a good-natured compliance than moral depravity, bringing such melancholy consequences in its wake. If schoolmasters could do anything to alter the strange code which exists almost instinctively among boys, so merciless to sins against honour, so heedless of sins against morality, and to cultivate social indignation against offences against purity, the battle would be nearly won.

Alarmists would have one believe that public schools are honeycombed with vice, and that all boys must pass through a fiery ordeal. I can only say that I was for two years at a very large private school, in days when the tone was undeniably worse than it is now, and never heard even the faintest hint of moral evil; at the public school where I spent seven years I never came into contact with the smallest temptation of a direct nature to evil, though I do not deny that I heard conversations of a Rabelaisian character; and this was the experience of many of my own contemporaries. Indeed, speaking with utter and entire frankness, I will say that I have good reasons for believing that things are far better now at public schools than they were twenty years ago. Each man can only appeal to his own experience, but my own experience is that the evil is not very widespread, but tends to gather in small groups. Of course, a boy in search of evil will probably be able to find it; but there is no reason why a boy who is pure-minded and manly should ever find a serious difficulty in his path.

Fifty years ago it would have been said that bullying, the tyranny of the strong over the weak, was an evil inseparable from school life; but bullying has now practically disappeared. There is, of course, some teasing, and the eccentric are ridiculed, if not oppressed, but it is not a danger which requires special vigilance.

At one public school the evil of which I have been speaking was practically exterminated under the guidance of a strong and sensible headmaster. And I say confidently that I look forward to a time, not necessarily very far distant, when the evil may be so far diminished as to become simply abnormal. That is all that can be hoped for, and that I dare to hope.

# XVI

# DEVOTION

My object has been in this little book to show that there should be a conscious consecration of self to work in schoolmasters. Not a sentimental consecration, and not a consecration to be talked about, but a serious and inner devotion to a life which holds the happiness of many other lives in its hand. It is not a thing to be brandished in the face of others. I have heard of a schoolmaster who went up the Matterhorn in the holidays, of whom a witty colleague said that he supposed it was because he was so fond of taking higher ground. It is a pity to be always waving motives about; it is not characteristically English, and it leads to a suspicion of priggishness which is apt to maim a man's influence. Of course, there have been great and high-minded schoolmasters who have undeniably been prigs. Dr Arnold was a man of this type, of great nobility and earnestness of character; but I am inclined to think that his lack of the humour which is inconsistent with priggishness, was a hindrance and not a help to his work. Of course, Dr Arnold, by sheer force of character and by intense seriousness, made a revolution in English schools, and perhaps such a revolution could hardly have been effected by anyone who was less candidly and frankly high-minded. The *Life of Dr Arnold* is an extremely inspiring book. The vigour of the man, his goodness, his simplicity, shine out on every page, but I think that it is easier to admire in a book than it would have been in real life, and there was a certain precocity which he developed in the men who came under his influence which was not wholly good. Sir George Trevelyan in a very witty book, *The Competition Wallah*, speaks of the influence which a young Civil Servant may find thrust into his hands, as only comparable to that arrogated

83

to himself by one of Dr Arnold's præposters in his first term at the University. The frame of mind which resolves definitely to exert influence over other people may have beneficial results, but it is a self-righteous and Pharisaical frame of mind; and the normal human being is more amenable to influence that is less consciously exerted and more simply displayed.

I have known several very effective schoolmasters who were certainly prigs, but I think that they would have been more effective still if this leaven had not permeated their excellent work.

The consecration of which I speak should be rather deep and secret; a man should aim at ruling and stimulating himself rather than at ruling and stimulating others. He should accept the inevitable failures and humiliations of school life as lessons sent to himself to show that he cannot always be as effective as he would like to be, to help in cleansing him from his secret faults. A prig in spirit is likely to put down his failures more to the fault of other people than to his own inadequacy.

I do not think that the temptations to a master to be priggish are very strong at present. I would rather believe that the tendency is the other way, and that the master is apt to think of himself as an ordinary professional man bent on doing work, which is often tiresome and not always valuable, in a conscientious way; – and this is not a very exalted frame of mind.

A man who had been recently appointed to a headmastership once went to see an elderly veteran who presided over a large school. The veteran gave him several hints, among which was to limit his school business strictly to school hours, "and then at six o'clock," he said, "you are a gentleman." "And what are you till then?" said the other grimly. It is this sense of trying to get rid of the consciousness of one's profession altogether in hours off duty that I deprecate. A master of my acquaintance, who was keenly alive to the social disabilities of his trade, was reduced to saying to his fashionable friends who asked him what he had been doing, that he had been staying in Bedfordshire. This is, of course, an extreme and exaggerated instance, but it represents a frame of mind in which good work can hardly be done, and which is not unknown among schoolmasters.

The schoolmaster should consider himself as vowed for a time to a species of monastic life. If he is a man of strong preferences he will find abundance of self-discipline in the punctual bells, the round of simple and often distasteful duties, in the constant necessity that he will be under of laying down something that he desires to do in order to take up something which he does not desire to do. But he should try to realise that these are not interruptions to life, but, for him, life itself; and that he must accept them as part of the conditions of life, as a definite training which is sent to him in this world.

As an old judge once said in my presence with great solemnity: "The judge who does not repress the first symptoms of irritability which inevitably occur during the examination of a stupid or unsatisfactory witness is lost. Irritability only hampers justice." So the schoolmaster is lost who does not cheerfully accept interruption as a necessary part of his life.

Then, too, the schoolmaster must reflect upon the gravity of his charge. He is there to turn boys, if he can, into good citizens; to curb, to correct, but also to encourage and to lift. And if he cannot feel the beauty and the solemnity of the charge, 'Feed My lambs', which he receives as certainly as the apostle of old, he is out of place as a schoolmaster. If he looks upon himself as a sophist or as a gaoler, his view will be either cynical or rigid; rigidity is bad, but cynicism is far worse, and yet it is not uncommon to see a man drifting into cynicism as he goes on, teaching things in the value of which he does not believe, looking upon boys as necessary evils, thinking only of how to get through his work with as little friction and fatigue as possible. If a man finds such a mood growing upon him, I can only say that I believe it to be a plain duty for him to stand aside and to yield his place to one who will bring to the task a little more hopefulness and generosity and enthusiasm.

One thing is certain, that schoolmastering cannot be looked upon in a frivolous spirit. I do not mean that there should be a heavy cloud of duty and rectitude over every schoolmaster's mind, but it will not do to talk of it as a profession like any other, which a man must practise to live. Of course in all other professions other people are dependent on you to a certain extent. The employer of labour must have the welfare of the employed at heart; the officer must be interested in his men; but the schoolmaster's duty and *raison d'être* is to make something definite out of the minds and bodies and souls of the children committed to him. A man who as a schoolmaster is careless or idle or indifferent may be quite certain that he is doing active harm, and that the Gospel warning as to what is the position of the man who offends one of these little ones is addressed directly to him. It is of no use to deceive oneself in the matter; the man who is a lazy teacher, who is a careless tutor, who has a bad house, is imperilling the bodies and souls of the boys whom he professes to guide and guard. A careless housemaster may reflect that by his carelessness corruption may flow year after year into many souls, which under better influence might have been pure and good and strong. No solemnity of words is needed to make such a statement impressive; it is the hard literal fact. Even a conscientious, anxious, diligent master may have much to reproach himself with; but for a man to pursue such a trade without principles, without purpose, and without conviction, is a great and heinous sin, and deserves the punishment which such sins receive.

One of the singular things about education is this, that whenever one looks back to any period one sees that gross and discreditable things were done and permitted by schoolmasters, which one cannot see how decent or conscientious men could allow to continue. Not to travel far for instances, no doubt the Eton masters of the last century, the Fellows of the college, were virtuous and even godly men; but they let continue under their eyes a state of things in Long Chamber which was a positive disgrace to civilisation. "Now, please God, I will do something for those poor boys," was what good Provost Hodgson said as his carriage drew up at the lodge at Eton, under the walls of Long Chamber, when he came to take possession. Of course the parent shares the responsibility with the schoolmaster to a certain extent; but people are slow to move, and parents will allow their boys to continue in a house where they know that an evil tone exists, rather than remove the boy from the school, and much rather than repeat to the schoolmaster what they hear, for fear that unpopularity and persecution should fall on the boy, vaguely hoping that it will be all right in the end. These are some of the dark abysses of life; but schoolmasters may well ask themselves what there is in their present handling of affairs which will be looked upon by the next generation as preposterous or shameful. I think it probable that our present system will not appear conspicuously barbarous to the educators of fifty years hence, because the whole matter is being anxiously and carefully studied by many conscientious schoolmasters everywhere; but I have no doubt at all that there are points to which we are blind, that will rouse the wonder and wrath of good men after us. And therefore we ought to labour to get rid of prejudice and traditional feeling in the matter, and to try and see things in a wise and liberal spirit. The difficulties are great because the boys with whom we have to deal are very tenacious of custom, very limited in view, very blind to their own best interests. The work must, I believe, be individual more than comprehensive; and the best cure for the evils of school life is that men should flow into the profession who have a strong sense of duty and vocation, a large fund of affection and pity and patience, strong common sense, tranquillity, and width of view.

The object of this little book will have been attained if it induces a few men to look at their profession in a different light, to try to modify their views and to clarify their ideal. It is not written from the point of view of one who has succeeded in doing this, but from the point of view of one who feels keenly his own inadequacy and failure, but would like to do better.

If the responsibility is great, the reward is great. A schoolmaster at the end of his career can look back upon an active, wholesome life, and need never question the usefulness of what he has been doing, even though he may lament that it was not better done. He must not look to great monetary rewards or large recognition of his work. He must acquiesce if the boys, to whom he seemed in their tender years so great and effective a man, come back and find him a tiresome, *borné* person with a narrow horizon and a limited stock of ancient stories. But he will have made many very real friends, and have met with much gratitude, which he will be conscious of not having deserved. He may look back to having given his life to a noble work, and he may be abundantly thankful if he has made a few feeble feet firmer, caused a few timorous natures to be braver and stronger, helped a few boys to resist or conquer grave faults, and ruled a small community with diligence and harmony and happiness. He may have an abundant stock of bright memories, tender thoughts, and beautiful experiences; and he will be a very hard and dull person if he is not a little wiser, a little more thrilled with the mysterious wonder of life, a little more conscious of the vast and complex design of the world in which he has been permitted to play a real part.

# Other titles from Peridot Press

### *The Following Game,*
### Jonathan Smith

ISBN 978 1 908095 01 5

A follow-up to Jonathan's acclaimed 2002 book *The Learning Game*, this
is a book about cricket, family and poetry; it's about a father following
a son's career in the public eye and the close relationship they share.
Jonathan Smith was, for many years, head of English at Tonbridge
School. As well as *The Learning Game*, he has published six novels and
written many plays for radio. He is the father of the writer Ed Smith,
who played cricket for Kent, Middlesex and England.

### *The Lanchester Tradition,*
### G F Brady

ISBN 0 901577 92 8

Although G F Bradby's classic tale first appeared a few short months
before the outbreak of the First World War, it remains one of the best
stories of school life ever written. While it is about a school, in essence
it is about change and institutional fear of change, and so should be
required reading for Heads.

### *The Lighter Side of Life,*
### Ian Hay

ISBN 1 904724 42 6

Ian Hay's renowned book about school life, first published in 1914,
links traditions established in the times of Arnold and Thring with the
echoes of them that have persisted until modern times.
Written when he was a schoolmaster, the author went on to be an
eminent soldier and playwright as well as author.

**To order these and other John Catt titles, please go to:**
**www.johncattbookshop.com**